Suicide: *The Forever Decision*

D1059183

Suicide
The Forever Decision
...

For Those
Thinking about Suicide,
and for Those
Who Know, Love,
or Counsel Them

PAUL G. QUINNETT

New Expanded Edition

CROSSROAD • NEW YORK

This Printing: December 2016

The Crossroad Publishing Company
www.crossroadpublishing.com

Printed in the United States of America

Library of Congress Cataloging-in-Publication Data

Quinnett, Paul G., 1939–
  Suicide : the forever decision.

  1. Suicide.   2. Suicide—Prevention.   3. Suicide—
Psychological aspects.   I. Title.
HV6545.Q85   1987   616.85′844505   87-9064
ISBN 0-8245-1352-5 (pbk.)

Disclaimer

Both author and publisher wish the reader to know that this book does not offer mental health treatment, and in no way should be considered a substitute for consultation with a professional.

*   *   *

The identities of the people written about in this book have been carefully disguised in accordance with professional standards of confidentiality and in keeping with their rights to privileged communication with the author.

Contents

Introduction

Dear Reader,

I don't know who you are or why you are reading these words. I only know that you have picked up this book and, for the moment, are reading it. It is my hope that if you need this book, you will continue to read it.

As an author, it would help me a great deal if I knew more about you. But I don't and, unless we meet sometime someplace, we can never know one another. So we are stuck right here in the beginning. We are strangers and that is the way things will be between us. But this should not stop us. At least it will not stop me.

I am going to write this book directly to you, as if you were sitting with me in my office. My office is a warm room. It is quiet and private. We have comfortable chairs and the phone doesn't ring. No one will disturb us in my office. It is the office in which I do what psychologists often do—listen to people, talk with them, try to help them with life's problems.

At the outset I must assume a couple of things about you. And while it is dangerous to make assumptions about people, because of our relationship, I will have to do it. I will assume that because you are reading this book, you have thought about taking your own life, or that you have already attempted to do so. Either way, I will assume you are greatly troubled and that you have considered ending your life.

Assuming this to be true, I am going to talk to you about the pain of living and the consequences of dying, so far as I know about them. I am going to talk to you about suicide. And because your life is at stake, I am not going to fool around. I am not going to kid you. I am not going to mince words. Rather, I intend to be just as honest and straightforward as I know how to be.

And because I have known many people who have wanted to kill themselves and too many who have, I have some idea of what kind of mood you are in at the moment. I know you may not be up to reading a book. But maybe you could read this one. I will keep it short.

One of the reasons I have written this book is that suicide is an unpleasant topic. People do not like to talk about it. They do not like to hear that another human being is so troubled that he is considering self-destruction. But this silence is not good for us. It is not good for the troubled person and it is not good for those of us who may wish to avoid the fact that someone we know is so desperate and so alone that ending his life seems the only solution to his problems. It is time we talked, and talked candidly.

Some people may argue that a book of this kind should not be written and that, somehow, talking plainly about suicide will increase the chances that a reader may kill himself. I do not believe this is true.

Rather, it is my feeling that the more we learn about dying, the more we learn about living. And, when we have learned more about both, maybe we are better able to fully live all of the life we have left to us.

Another reason I have written this book is that many people kill themselves without ever knowing that help was just a phone call away. You wonder, in this modern age, how this can be. But it is true. So maybe this book will find its way into the hands of someone who never knew help was there and where to find it. Maybe this book will give someone that little bit of courage they need to ask for that help, or to hold on for another day or another week or until their life changes for the better and the thoughts of suicide begin to fade.

Just one more note. I do not have any magic answers or quick solutions to life's problems. I don't think anyone does. So I won't offer you any easy ways of living or simple solutions to the pain and suffering that seem to be a part of all our lives. But because this book is about suicide and nothing less than your life is at stake, I won't apologize for what I have to say to you that you may not like. For all I know, this book may be the last thing you ever read.

Paul Quinnett

1 ————————————— ...

You Don't Have to Be Crazy

The first thing I want to tell you about suicide is that you don't have to be crazy to think about it or, for that matter, even to try it. Suicide *is* a solution. No matter what anyone tells you, suicide does solve problems, at least *your* problems. And if you succeed, it solves them once and for all. As you have no doubt already figured out, once you are dead nothing can hurt you anymore. Once you are dead you are beyond feeling bad. Once you are dead you can't possibly care what happens anymore. Whatever pain you are in, it will end just as soon as you stop breathing. Since there is no point in kidding each other right here in the beginning, I won't argue with you that suicide doesn't work. It does. Or at least it seems to.

Before this time in your life, my guess is that when you heard people say they felt like killing themselves, you thought they were crazy. Now, if you are in that same place, maybe you can see how they felt. For whatever reasons people think it, most of them will say you are crazy for thinking about suicide. Or, if you kill yourself, they will say you must have been crazy to have done it.

But the truth is most people who kill themselves are not mentally ill, at least in the formal sense. Not at all. Most people who kill themselves are people just like you and me; people who, for reasons I hope you will explore with me, have decided that life is just not worth living anymore. The great majority of people who attempt or complete a suicide are so sad or hopeless or angry that they simply can't stand it anymore. Or they have been dealt such a terrible blow by life that they are overwhelmed and can see no other way to end the feeling of loss and loss of control over their future. But they are not crazy. And, most likely, neither are you.

Later in this book I will talk in detail about depression, loneliness, anger, hopelessness, stress, and how these states of mind can influence us and trigger our thoughts of suicide. But for the moment I would encourage you to try to read the book through from front to back so that you will understand the hows, the whys, and all the risks and consequences of trying to kill yourself.

One of the things that happens when you begin to think about suicide as a way out is that you begin to feel better, sometimes a little better, sometimes a lot better. After all, when you've been stuck with a problem for which there seems to be no answer, finally finding one is a great relief. You might ask, "How can this be?"

Because we humans are capable of imagining things we have never done or being in places we have never been, we are all capable of imagining what it might be like to be dead, or at least what it might be like not to be alive. Only man is capable of imagining his own death. We can play our death out like a role in a movie. We can close our eyes and see ourselves lying lifeless in a casket. And, whether we will admit it or not, just about all of us at some time or another, have imagined what it would be like to be dead.

It is this powerful ability to imagine an end to our problems that makes thinking about suicide possible. And it isn't like anyone can stop us from thinking about taking our own lives. It is *our* mind, *our* imagination, *our* ability to anticipate what death might be like that makes us human and no one, but no one, can stop us from being human.

From my point of view, you have every right to think about

suicide as a way to solve whatever problem you are dealing with right now. Suicide is a decision every single human being has. Sometimes it is our only decision. And sometimes, for some people, at least in my view, maybe it is the right decision.

But for the moment, I'd like to put the suicide decision on the shelf and ask you to stay with me for the rest of this book. As you can guess, I'm not writing this book to hurry anyone along. Rather, I'm writing this book to help you examine suicide in some detail and maybe in some ways that haven't yet occurred to you.

I have one other belief I need to share with you right now. That belief is simply this: Every time any of us has to make a decision, we always make the very best decision we can. None of us starts out to solve a problem and says, "I think I'll make a lousy decision this time." In my view, this never happens. What does happen is that each time we have to make a decision, we take all the available information we have, run it through our little brains and then, sometimes crossing our fingers, we decide what we will do. And herein lies the problem.

What if we didn't have all the information necessary to make a really good decision? How many times have you looked back at a decision you made and said, "Gee, I shouldn't have done that. I didn't know it would turn out that way. How could I have been so stupid?" If you are like me, then you've done this hundreds of times, maybe thousands. No one has a corner on the stupidity market and making decisions you later regret is just part of being human.

Among other things, life requires that each of us makes decisions, hundreds of them each day. There are little decisions like what to wear to work or school each morning, and big decisions like what to do in life, whom to marry or whether, when things are going badly, even to go on living. Everyone has to make the same decisions. The trouble is that we never seem to have all the information we need to make the best possible decision every single time. If we did, we'd make perfect decisions. But since we don't, we keep on making imperfect decisions, decisions that we later regret. Frankly, I don't see anyway out of this for any of us.

But there is hope. As people get older they generally get a little smarter. They get a little smarter because the longer they live, the more information they have and the better the decisions they tend to make. Think back to when you were a kid. Think back to a decision you made that, given what you know now, you would never make again.

For example, if you are a smoker, given what you now know about smoking, would you have tried that first cigarette? Probably not. Or maybe you got into a fight with a best friend or a parent and decided never to speak to them again. Would you act in exactly the same way today? Maybe not. The point is, we can all look back and regret some of our decisions. We can all look back and see that we were stupid, or maybe ignorant is a better word. Ignorance (not having all the facts) is what most of us are most of the time. But this is okay with me. I don't mind being ignorant. I don't like being embarrassed because I don't know something, but then nobody ever promised me I'd always know everything I needed to know when I needed to know it. And, unless you got a different guarantee than I did, I don't imagine you're any better off.

But I think we can, all of us, hope that each day we will get a little smarter. And I have always felt that if I can look back at some dumb decision I made and say to myself, "Paul, that was a stupid decision," then at least I'm not getting any dumber.

So what has all this to do with suicide? What it has to do with suicide is, that when people start thinking about ending their own life, they generally don't have all the facts. They may think they do, but they don't. And, because suicide is such a permanent solution and one you can't go back and remake, then for your own sake, you ought to make the decision only after you have considered all the facts.

And I mean every single one.

One thing I have learned from people who have thought about

suicide and finally decided to do it is that once they've made their mind up, they suddenly feel better. In fact, some of them have told me they feel wonderful. "Now I know what to do," they have said. And this is exactly what happens to any of us once we have finally found a solution to a problem we've been struggling with. It is as if we have set down a huge burden and, in setting it down, we feel a great relief.

But just one minute. Sure, suicide will stop the hurting. Suicide will make all the problems go away. Suicide will end the nightmare. But is it really as simple as all that? Isn't it a bit scary? And isn't it final?

You might think that last question is a silly one. Of course suicide is final. But you might be surprised to learn that the younger a person is, the less he knows about death and the finality of death. But the older you get, the more death you see and, in the process, you come to know that a successful suicide attempt is truly the end of life. As a friend of mine who works with suicidal young people recently said, "Some kids think suicide is a fad. They have a big problem and they say, 'I think I'll try suicide this week. If it doesn't work, I'll try something else next week.'"

Next week!!?

If I have a job ahead of me in this book it is, more than anything else, to convince you that what looks like a quick and easy solution actually isn't all that quick and easy. As often as not, suicide is a complicated, messy business and creates as many problems as it solves. True, you don't have to be crazy to think about it or maybe even try it but, if you'll forgive the joke, suicide can be dangerous to your health.

2 _____ ...

An Idea That Kills

What I want to talk to you about in this chapter is just where you got the idea of taking your own life in the first place. It didn't just pop into your head one day from out of nowhere. But since I can't ask you where you got the notion, I'm going to have to do my best to help you figure this out for yourself.

Take a minute right now and ask yourself, "When did I first start thinking about taking my own life?"

Now ask yourself, "Have I known anyone who committed suicide?"

Because human beings learn a great deal from each other, all of us are subject to examples set for us by people we know, by strangers, and by famous people. We learn which fork to pick up at a formal dinner by watching the person next to us. We learn what to wear to the dance by watching what other people wear to dances. Most of us cut our hair long or short depending on what most other people our age are doing with their hair.

For those of us who live in America, we all know Marilyn Monroe committed suicide. We know the novelist Ernest Hemingway killed himself. We read about people killing themselves all the time. And sometimes we think, "If someone like Marilyn Monroe, with all her beauty and money and success, can kill herself, why shouldn't I?"

Or maybe someone in our family committed suicide. If one of our parents committed suicide, then we might well ask ourselves, "If dad couldn't take it, how can I?"

Or maybe one of our best friends killed himself or herself. Or someone at school. If we look around our own hometown and read the papers or watch the news on TV, one thing is very obvious: people are killing themselves all the time. While not exactly a pastime, people all around us are making attempts on their lives. In the time it took you to read this paragraph someone, somewhere in America, has made an attempt to kill himself.

Americans, compared to most people in the world, are killing themselves off at a faster and faster pace. It is, according to some experts, an epidemic.

So, what does this tell us? What this tells us is that we got the *idea* of committing suicide from someone else. We didn't think of this solution all by ourselves. Suicide is hardly a new idea and people have been doing it for as long as there have been people. And so, if we somehow have got hold of the idea of committing suicide, then we must have got it from someone—a friend, a family member, a famous person. Someone, somewhere has shown us that suicide is something we too can do. And when someone else has shown us the way, is it easier for us to take the same route?

The research on this is very clear: When a famous person like Marilyn Monroe kills herself, the suicide rate rises. It is as if the people who had been thinking their lives' problems were insoluble saw, by Marilyn's example, that self-destruction was a real possibility. Maybe they said, "If it was good enough for Marilyn, it is good enough for me."

And when a Japanese teen idol recently killed herself by jumping to her death, at least six teenagers also killed themselves within just a few days. Some of them jumped and most left a note indicating they had taken their cue from her example.

The same thing happens closer to home. When one or two

kids in a high school kill themselves, more kids are likely to kill themselves. And if someone in a family commits suicide, the rest of the family members are more likely to commit suicide. Right or wrong, we all learn by example.

One suicidal man I worked with was very serious about ending his life. His wife had had an affair with another man, his kids were in trouble, and his job was not going well. I asked him where he got the idea of taking his own life. "Well," he said, "both of my parents committed suicide."

I had never met a man whose mother and father had both killed themselves. But I knew that whatever I might be able to say to him about why he should go on living, I was up against the two most powerful and influential people in his life, mom and dad.

"I was only five when they did it," he said. "So I don't think it bothered me too much."

But of course it had. As we worked together, he was able to tell me that every time he had faced a tough problem in life, the idea of committing suicide had crept into his mind, almost against his will. It was as if, despite his promise never to kill himself as his parents had, he could not stop thinking about it. And now that his life was going very badly, he could not keep the thoughts out any longer.

So in a way this man really had no chance to avoid thinking about suicide. It had been there since his first memories. It was as if his parents had given him a terrible gift. They had shown him that, when life becomes unbearable, this is what you do.

So I need to ask you once again, just where did you get the idea of taking your own life? Has someone who was close to you shown you the way? Has a parent or a grandparent or an uncle or an aunt or a friend set an example for you? Or have you compared your misery with someone whom you thought you knew and decided that if suicide was good enough for them, it is good enough for me?

If your answer is yes, then I will ask you one simple question:

Is your life, your problem, your particular pain, exactly like theirs? Are you an identical person in an identical crisis?

I think your answer has to be no. Because, like it or not, we are all entirely separate, entirely different, entirely unique human beings. There has never been anyone exactly like us on the planet before and there will never be anyone exactly like us on the planet in the future. However much we may not like ourselves or however much we may regret what we have done or have become, we are at least one-of-a-kind persons—the likes of which this world will never see again.

And, being such unique creatures, shouldn't we make our own unique decisions?

3 — ・・・

"Don't I Have a Right to Die?"

A lot of suicidal people I've worked with have asked me this question and, frankly, I don't have a very good answer. In a way, I'm glad I don't. But since I imagine you may have asked yourself this same question, I'm going to share with you what I have told others.

First, it is not for me, a psychologist, to say whether you have a right to die. There is nothing in my training or background or personal experience that gives me any special knowledge about the subject. I am not a minister or a priest or any kind of church authority. I am not a judge. If anything, I have been trained to save lives, not to help people end them.

At least from a legal point of view, I think I can give you a partial answer: No, you do not have an absolute right to kill yourself.

At this moment in the history of America it is still against the law to attempt suicide and if you try it, sometimes unpleasant legal consequences can follow. Although it rarely happens now, not so long ago people were put in jail for trying to kill themselves. But in the last few decades suicide has become less of a crime and more of a symptom that something is desperately wrong with people who try it and that, if given some help, they will give up the idea and get on with living.

Frankly, there is a great deal of confusion about this right-to-die business. On the one extreme are those people who argue no one has a right to die under any circumstances and, on the other extreme, are those who say all of us have a right to die any time we so choose, including by suicide.

Most of the right-to-die debate centers around the issue of whether a person who is terminally ill or very old and sick and not expected to improve with sometimes-painful treatments, has the right to refuse medical care. The basic questions are: Does a patient have the right to refuse lifesaving medical care if, in his case, he is going to die soon anyway? And, should he have a right to be assisted with his own suicide?

There are groups of people organized to push for legislation that would permit this sort of "death with dignity" for those who are terminally ill. While some might disagree, it seems to me that the goals of these groups are humane and none, so far as I know, argues for the right to suicide if you are young and healthy.

But unless you have recently gotten the word that you are terminally ill and about to die sometime in the near future, I'm going to assume that you are thinking about suicide for different reasons.

You might ask, "What happens if I attempt to kill myself and don't succeed?"

Every state in the fifty has some kind of involuntary-treatment law that permits a judge, on the basis of professional testimony, to put you in a hospital for treatment and to prevent you from making further attempts on your life. The state must prove you are mentally ill and therefore need treatment, but it can generally do this without all that much trouble. You lose, however temporarily, your civil rights when this happens.

As we have already discussed, however, you do not have to be mentally ill to take your own life. In fact, most people who do commit suicide are not legally "insane." So it seems we have a very interesting problem.

To prevent you from killing yourself, doctors like myself will stand up in court and say something to the effect that, by reason of a mental illness, you are a danger to yourself and need treatment. But—and this is the weird part—you may, in a matter of a few hours to a couple days, get up one morning and say, "I've decided not to kill myself, after all." And if you can convince us you mean what you say, you can leave the hospital and go home. Question: Are you now completely cured of your so-called mental illness?

Obviously not, since the chances are you were never "mentally ill" in the first place. But this doesn't mean you may not be depressed or angry or in a major life crisis and need counseling. Being detained in a hospital because of suicidal thinking or after making an attempt on your life only means that, in the opinion of people like me, you were so confused or off balance or upset that—at least at the time—you were in danger of making a very bad decision.

So, you have every right to ask, if I am not "crazy," why is thinking about suicide a symptom and, if it is a symptom, what is it a symptom of?

As I have said, I do not believe you have to be mentally ill to think about suicide. Research has shown that a substantial majority of people have considered suicide at one time in their lives, and I mean considered it seriously—maybe as seriously as you. And these were normal people, just as you are. I've talked to lots of people who have seriously considered suicide. Some of them say that at the time they were thinking about it they must have been "temporarily insane." Maybe that's as good an explanation as we need for now.

For the moment let's just accept the fact that, at the present time in America, it is not okay to try to kill yourself and that, if you try it, you can lose your freedom—at least for a while.

The people who have the authority to try to stop you from committing suicide are people like me: psychologists, psychiatrists, social workers, nurses, physicians, and all sorts of mental health and drug- and alcohol-treatment specialists. The police have responsibilities as well. These professionals, for lack of a better term, are called the mental-health system. And it is this "system," however good or bad, that you will come into contact with if you attempt suicide and do not succeed. If you succeed . . . well, I think you know what "system" takes care of your remains.

Here is a word of caution: For a lot of reasons I won't bore you with, you can't always count on the system to respond perfectly. If you make an attempt on your own life and fail, consider this:

Sometimes the police will investigate and take whatever action they think is necessary. They may take you to a hospital, or they may not. They may let you go on the promise you won't try to kill yourself again. They might even take you to jail, especially if you endangered someone else in your attempt.

If you go or are taken to a hospital by friend or family or the police, sometimes the doctors will treat you and let you go home. Sometimes they will admit you to a psychiatric ward in the hospital. Or, if they do not have a psychiatric ward, they may make arrangements to send you to a state mental hospital. It depends on the hospital and how the system works in your town or area.

Sometimes, if the doctors think you need inpatient psychiatric care and you are unwilling to go voluntarily, they will put you in a psychiatric facility even if you do not want to go. As I have mentioned, all states have laws on the books that permit them to do this. And, as I said, you can lose your freedom, at least for a time.

Now then, if you are reading a lot of "sometimes" as we go along here it is because, despite laws in every state designed to prevent suicide, these laws are never carried out in exactly the same way from one place to another or even from one day to the next. People in the system—psychologists, psychiatrists, emergency-room people, policemen and women, etc.—all have different opinions about people who attempt suicide. Some of them, to be honest, don't like people who try to kill themselves. Some of them would just as soon you would succeed and get it over with. Some people (and this should not be news to you) don't give a damn whether you live or die. I've heard some of them say, "They're going to do it sooner or later anyway, so why bother?"

My point is this: Attempting suicide is a risky business. And I don't mean that as a joke.

But there is one thing of which you can be sure; if you make an attempt on your own life and the proper authorities find out about it, they will take some kind of action. And if they believe you are serious about committing suicide, they are going to do every legal thing they can to stop you. Your reasons for wanting to die, even if they seem like very good ones to you, won't make any difference.

Right or wrong, you've got to look at it from our point of view. If we truly believe you represent a danger to yourself, we simply are not going to take your word that you won't try to hurt yourself again. We may not know you, but at least we know you are a fellow human being who is hurting so bad that you don't want to live any longer. And if we know this, we are not going to sit on our hands and do nothing.

I also need to warn you that even some mental health professionals do not agree about what action should be taken to try to stop a suicidal person from following through on his or her threat. Some professionals believe that each person, so long as he or she is not obviously insane, has the ultimate responsibility for living or dying. And so, should you happen upon one of these professionals, he may not pull out all the stops and see to it that you go to a hospital. He may agree with you that you have a right to die if you so choose and, if that's what you elect to do, then you are going to take all the responsibility for your own death.

But the great majority of professional helpers see any suicidal gesture or threat as serious and will do whatever they deem is necessary to try to stop you. If you're lucky, you'll meet professionals who really care.

And you should know, too, that doctors and counselors and hospitals and mental-health centers are getting sued all the time for making mistakes about suicidal people. If they know someone is suicidal and don't take all reasonable precautions, including hospitalizing the person against his will, and that person kills himself, then they are wide open for a lawsuit. So most of us do the conservative thing when we have an actively suicidal person on our hands; we lock him or her up. Whether this is always for "their own good" or "our own good," I can't say—maybe it is a bit of both.

In most states the authorities can keep you in a hospital against your will only so long—generally a few days to a few weeks. But if you keep trying to kill yourself, they will keep you just as long as they feel they need to. There is nothing that makes a mental-health person feel worse than to release a formerly suicidal patient from the hospital only to learn that he killed himself the next day.

From our side of it, we feel we are giving you a chance to consider other alternatives, get some help and rethink whether or not you really want to die. We know that most people who are considering the suicide decision will get better, their crisis will pass, and, sooner or later, they will want to live again. Knowing this, we will buy them some time—any way we can and even if they insist they don't want our help. It's as simple as that.

A couple of more notes on the right to die.

In ancient Greece, people who were considering suicide could go to the senate and make a case for why they should be permitted to end their own lives. If they could make a good enough case, they were permitted to take poison. No such higher governmental authority exists today.

Religions, by and large, have considered suicide a sin. Most still do. In our major religions the belief is that since God granted the miracle of life, only He can end it. And you, as one of His children, do not have the right to stop something God has started. Suicide is, therefore, a sin against God.

During the centuries that suicide was considered a sin, you could not be buried in sacred ground if you took your own life.

And in some places and times, a suicide's body was put on public display as a bad example, or simply tossed in a ditch outside of town. In our own country in the 1700s a suicide was often punished after the fact of his death. His property was confiscated, his family made to pay for his crime.

But in other cultures, suicide is not specifically against the law and, under special circumstances, even an honorable way to exit this life. The Japanese are the best known for acts of suicide, which, in their culture, are considered good and proper ways to leave this world.

And, finally, there are those people who sacrifice their own lives so that others may live: the soldier who throws himself on a hand grenade to save his buddies, the pilot who stays with his airplane to avoid hitting a schoolyard filled with children, and all sorts of people who knowingly put their lives in harm's way for the sake of others. These, to my way of thinking, are not so much acts of suicide as acts of heroism.

But here in America it is still not okay to try to kill yourself, especially if your reasons for wanting to do so are not considered sufficient. And even if they are very good reasons—you are in constant physical pain, you are going to die soon anyway, etc.— you may not be able to find anyone in authority who will take the responsibility to say, yes, you can end your own life.

But I can hear you thinking, "What the hell does he know? He doesn't know how I feel. He doesn't know what I've been through. And he can't possibly know what's best for me."

Well, you've got me there. Everything you may have just thought is absolutely true. I don't know you. I don't know your circumstances. I don't know what is best for you.

But I do know one thing: If you kill yourself, this one-way conversation is finished and so is every other conversation you may ever have. And once you are gone, it won't matter much whether you had a right to die or not.

So for now let's agree about something. Let's agree that even though suicide is against the civil laws of the land and against whatever God you may believe in and against what your friends and family believe in, you and I both know that you can still kill yourself. If you really want to end your own life, you can. I certainly can't stop you, your friends can't stop you, your parents can't stop you, and the police can't stop you. Even if they put you in a hospital for a few days to a few weeks, you can always stop talking about suicide and promise the doctors you won't do it and then, when they let you out, you can go ahead and kill yourself.

So, you and I both know something. We know that when we get right down to it, there is only one person who can decide whether you will live or you will die. And it isn't me. Right?

Right.

4   . . .

Are You Absolutely Sure?

When I told a friend I was writing this book he said, "Well, I guess as long as they continue reading it, they haven't made a final decision to die."

And so, since I still have your attention, I am going to assume that you haven't made the ultimate decision just yet. Or maybe even if you have, you might be willing to reconsider. As someone once said of the person who had really and finally and once-and-for-all made up his mind to kill himself, "He died ten minutes ago."

What I hope is true of you at this moment is that you are still uncertain about taking your own life. And because I have talked to hundreds of suicidal people, I can make a pretty good guess that you, even in your darkest hour, remain torn between ending your life or trying to go on with it. This is as it should be and, though it may not make you feel any better, almost all people considering suicide remain unsure about taking their own lives — even up to the moment they make an attempt. I can still remember interviewing a woman who had jumped from a bridge into a rushing river and survived. She had worn her raincoat because, as she put it, "I didn't want to get wet."

If I can make another guess about what has been going on inside your head and heart, it is that you have had long and difficult discussions with yourself about whether to live or die. In the psychology business, we call this ambivalence.

Ambivalence simply means that a person is struggling with a decision, examining the positive and negative aspects of some act or other and trying to anticipate the best possible outcome. It means having two opposite feelings at the same time—you want to do something and you don't want to do it. Sometimes dying seems the best thing to do, sometimes living seems the best thing to do. This ambivalence, as you well know, is a terrible thing to endure. It is a precarious balance of life against death and thinking about it saps all your energy. Ambivalence comes and goes, like a painful toothache.

I don't want to lecture you about the psychology of ambivalence or what it means, but I do want you to know that being uncertain about the decision to kill yourself is perfectly natural and that even though you may feel you are driving yourself crazy by talking to yourself about taking your own life, such self-talk is necessary, maybe essential.

The thing that concerns me most about your ambivalence is that it is as if your desire to live is on one side of a delicate balance scale, and your desire to die on the other. Both strong desires, they are balanced just so and neither of us knows, right now, what it might take to tip the scales in one direction or the other.

I would worry for you if, for example, a letter you were expecting did not come today. Such a disappointment, while very small in itself, might tip the scales in a negative direction. On the other hand, that phone call from someone you love might come through tonight, tipping the scales in the other direction, and everything would change for the better. This is what is scary about ambivalence and the delicate balancing act you may be experiencing.

I think that most everyone who has at one time thought about suicide is stronger for having thought about it. They have examined the death option in some detail and have, after weighing things out, decided that as tough as life is, it is still worth living. As one young man told me, "I thought about suicide once, even loaded the pistol. But then I realized I was too much of a coward to pull the trigger."

"A coward?" I asked him.

"Well, I guess I was afraid to die just then," he said. "Although I am not afraid of death now. After all, I looked death right in the eye."

Maybe, until we look death right in the eye, we cannot live life so well. And maybe, after we have done so, we are stronger for it. Maybe only after we have come close to death, can we come close to life. To me, it seems so.

You might look at your ambivalence this way: because none of us has ever been dead, it is easier to be negative about life (something we know about), than to be positive about death (something we don't know about). And it is only when we are confronted with our own deaths that death loses its promise to be better.

There is a story about a man who jumped into a river to kill himself but failed. While he was bobbing along in the current a police officer threw him a rope so that he could save himself. The man refused to take the rope. The officer then pulled his pistol and aimed it at the man, threatening to shoot him. The man, faced with a more certain death and the true negativity of it, grabbed the rope.

It might help for you to know that for every person who has made up his or her mind and has no doubts about ending his or her life, there are dozens more like you who remain unsure, uncertain, and hesitant. And if you were in my office with me, that is the way I would hope you would be. I would hope that the two of us would have the courage to look death square in the eye and not be afraid to talk about it. Because if we could do this we might begin to see that dying is something we all have to do someday and by talking about it we might come to a better understanding of what life is and what we can do with the days we have left.

Gambling with Death—the Most Dangerous Game

When we are in pain and having trouble making the decision to live or die, we sometimes flirt with death. We toy with suicide. We do things that may kill us, but we don't take full responsibility for what might happen. We say to ourselves, "If I die, so be it." Or, "If I survive, I guess I wasn't meant to die this time." This is like tossing a fatal coin—heads I live, tails I die.

I remember a young man named Joe who drove his car as fast as it would go along a twisting mountain road. He was angry and hurt that his girlfriend had left him for someone else. He was thinking he might be better off dead. He skidded around corners at high speeds and eventually crashed. His car was totaled, but he survived. When I saw Joe in the hospital, he said, yes, maybe he had been suicidal.

"Did you want to die?" I asked him.

"I don't know. I guess so."

"Do you want to die now?"

"Of course not," Joe said. "That was stupid. Now my insurance rates will go up." Then he laughed and said he had been sure to buckle up his seat belt before he headed into the mountains, ". . . just in case." This is ambivalence.

Even though I have said you do not have to be crazy to think about suicide, to my way of thinking this sort of gambling with death *is* crazy. It is like the person who loads a revolver with one bullet, spins the cylinder, points the muzzle to his head and pulls the trigger. It is like saying, I don't know if I really want to die, but I'll give death a chance. Or there is the person who takes a handful of sleeping pills, not knowing if there are enough pills to do the job. She may wake up or she may not. She will turn the matter over to fate.

To me at least, these are terrible gambles and even though I know how someone may despair of living, to give one's only life over to chance may be the worst solution of all.

(I will talk more about what can happen if you fail in a suicide attempt in a later chapter.)

Being unsure about wanting to die is okay and normal for people in a suicidal crisis and I don't want you to think for one minute that this uncertainty is anything that will go quietly away in a day or two. But it does go away. Most people in these desperate hours of ambivalence feel as though time has stopped or is barely moving. It is as if the rest of the world is going off at a normal clip, but for you, time has ground to a halt. And until things begin to change, it might help to know that what you are experiencing is what others in your same frame of mind have experienced. It is just the way it is.

There is one other thing of which I want you to be aware: suicidal logic. When you are in that trapped feeling of nowhere to go and stuck with the ambivalence of living or dying, you may think you are thinking clearly. Chances are you are not. Chances are you are depressed, and depressed people sometimes do not think so clearly or so well. (I have written more about depression in a later chapter.)

Consider this thought: "Either my life improves, or I must kill myself."

If this sample of thinking sounds familiar, ask yourself, "Is this the only way things can turn out, either A or B?" If your answer is yes, then you are stuck in a kind of one-way logic. And a dangerous one at that.

Just for the moment, I will agree with you that maybe your life won't improve, that things will go on being miserable and hopeless and that, if you're depressed, your depression will go on forever. Option A, your life getting better is out.

Question: Do you really have to take option B and kill yourself?

Answer: Well, not necessarily.

There is always option C. With option C you could, for example, just go on being depressed and miserable. People do it all the time.

What is illogical about suicidal thinking is that you have given yourself only two ways to go with your problems—up or down, life or death. Maybe you hadn't thought of option C, just to go on being miserable.

Remember, the only person who says that if life does not improve I have to kill myself, is you.

Here is another dangerous piece of suicidal logic. We call it circular logic. This in-the-head conversation goes like this:

"I'm going to kill myself."

"Why?"

"Because my problems can't be solved."

"How do you know your problems can't be solved?"

"Are you nuts? If my problems could be solved, do you think I'd be on the verge of killing myself?"

This kind of logic is like having one shoe nailed to the floor and running at top speed: the faster you go, the dizzier you get. It never occurs to you to sit down, untie your shoes, step out of them, and walk off barefoot in some new direction.

Sometimes it takes talking to someone besides yourself to break out of circular logic, someone who is on the outside looking in.

I know that such examples of suicidal logic will not do you much good and that, of all the things that might improve your situation or mood, the least helpful thing I could say would be something like, "Cheer up, you have everything to live for!" So I won't say that.

But I want you to know that if you let some average person know you are thinking about killing yourself, this "cheer up" message is pretty much what you can expect them to say to you. This is their logical argument to try to counter your logical argument. Their argument is just as simpleminded as yours. Unfortunately, when you are despairing of living another day, either kind of logic isn't much worth a damn.

There is the old joke where someone is trying to cheer up a depressed person and says, "Cheer up, things could be worse!"

The depressed person cheered up and, sure enough, things got worse.

So I won't kid you that it is an easy thing to think your way out of a suicidal crisis and quickly end the ambivalence that haunts you. After all, you may have finally arrived at the point where you've begun to think seriously about suicide after a long and losing battle, a battle I can never know about.

Disappointments can mount up and maybe you have been nickel-and-dimed to death. Or maybe you have lost greatly and just can't imagine doing without what you have lost. Either way, once the suicidal crisis starts it isn't like I (or anyone else) can say, "Bingo! Your crisis is over!"

On the other hand, I want you to know that no crisis lasts forever and that being unsure about dying is okay and normal until things begin to change. And, if you don't kill yourself first, things *will* change—sometimes even for the better.

5 ⸻⸻⸻⸻⸻⸻⸻ • • •

One Step Back, Please

Because of the way I have chosen to write this book, I am going to make another assumption about you; I'm going to guess that if you have been thinking about suicide, then you've also been thinking about how to do it. Sooner or later, when any of us gets into this frame of mind, we begin to consider just how we would actually do it. Suicide is not only the ultimate decision, it is also the ultimate "how-to" project.

But since I can't guess where you might be in your thinking, I'm going to have to make some educated guesses. I'm going to ask you to consider doing something—not for me, but for yourself.

Let me back up just one moment. It is not an easy thing to kill a human being. Even if you plan to do the job yourself, you have to give some thought as to just how you will do it. In my business we call this subject the method. And when we are working with a suicidal person, we will ask, "How do you plan to take your life?"

If the person says, "I don't know yet," we consider the risk much lower than if the person says, "With a .45 automatic pistol on Friday afternoon at three o'clock."

In a word, the clearer the plan the higher the risk.

Since I can't possibly know what sort of plan you might be considering or where you are on a possible timetable, I have a suggestion that may sound a little screwy. (If you've always thought that psychologists were pretty screwy anyway, here's some proof.)

What I want to ask you to do, at least for now, is to take one little step back from the suicide decision. This doesn't mean you can't go ahead later, but for now, for today at least, take one small step back from the brink. You can flush those pills you've been saving down the toilet or give your gun to a friend or throw the razor blades out or stop going to a high bridge or building while you try to think things through. In a word, do whatever you need to do to reduce the availability of the means by which you might want to take your life.

The reason I ask you to do this is simple—any of us can be tempted by a perfect opportunity. I know that when we are confused or unhappy or angry, it is even more difficult to resist temptation and so, if we put what is tempting us out of sight or out of reach, it is as if we have put a bit of time between us and our impulses. And, once you have taken one step back, sometimes you can see things differently. Sometimes you can't, but sometimes you can.

From talking with many people who have tried to kill themselves I know that once a suicidal person puts a plan in motion, it is sometimes very difficult for him to stop the forward momentum. I have even had people tell me that, at just the last minute before they tried to kill themselves, it seemed as if they had to go ahead and try. "After all," one of them said, "I'd gone so far I couldn't turn back."

Maybe it would help to think of things this way. None of us is going to get out of this world alive. The clock is ticking against all of us. So, it is never a matter of "if" you will die, but rather only a matter of *how* and *when*.

That statement may sound a little grim, but then it isn't like we aren't talking about serious issues here. Try as we might, none of us can avoid this business of dying. It isn't like the comedian Woody Allen once joked, "I'm not afraid of dying. . . . I just don't want to be there when it happens." No. Dying is the one appointment none of us gets to cancel.

Many people who are thinking about suicide have decided that, if they can control nothing else in their lives, at least they can take control of the how and when of their dying. This feeling of being in control is a good one, very much like the first time you learned to ride a bike without training wheels. And this sense of being in control of our own destiny is very important to us, so important that many people who take their own lives do so in order to reaffirm that, in fact, they are in control of at least something.

But the bad thing about suicidal plans that have been put in motion is that they can sometimes take on a power of their own, a power over which the person himself loses control. Suicide may be the ultimate exercise of personal power, but it should never become an obligation.

A young mother I knew once planned to kill herself on the same day of her daughter's death. Her teenage daughter had died of cancer the year before. The mother's husband had left her and she had been miserable and unhappy and had wanted to die for several months. In her thinking about dying, she had decided it would be fitting and proper for her to die on the same day as her daughter. But as the day drew closer and her life took a turn for the better, she felt less and less like killing herself.

"But I promised myself I would do it on the fourteenth," she said. "And a promise is a promise."

Luckily for her, she wasn't such a good promise keeper that she couldn't break at least this one.

And there was something else to this story. In the woman's private plans to end her life, she had promised her dead daughter she would join her on the fourteenth. When we talked this through, it turned out that when the lady put herself in her daughter's shoes, in fact, the daughter would not have wanted her to die. Relieved of this burden, the woman was able to re-make a different kind of promise.

Please understand that I am not telling you to give up your plans to die or your thoughts about how to do it. That would be silly of me. I can't control your thoughts and neither can anyone else. All I am asking is that you back up a bit, give yourself a little breathing room and a little time to mull things over.

Somewhere in the rest of this book you may find something that will help you change your mind. Or, in the next few hours or days or weeks, something may happen that you didn't expect, something that will give you reasons to live. So, for your own sake, please take one step back.

6   • • •

The Bug in the Cup

Now that we have a little more time together, in the next few chapters I want you to do some exploring with me. I want you to imagine, for the moment anyway, that for the last several weeks or months you have been like a bug trapped in the bottom of a cup. How you got in the cup, I don't know. How you will get out of the cup will be, most likely, a result of something you do, or what someone helps you to do. And, just maybe, I can help you a little.

The bug-in-the-cup idea is not mine, I got it from another psychologist who, in his lectures, used to use the example of a bug trapped in a cup to illustrate a major problem we all face from time to time: namely, that once we are trapped in a situation, our solutions are limited by what we can see. We have walked around and around inside our cup and, seeing no way out, we decide that all hope is finished and that we are forever trapped. We climb up, but slip back down. Everything we try fails. Then, when we are convinced there are no possible escapes left to us, we become depressed and helpless and hopeless and, sometimes, suicidal.

While human beings are bigger and supposedly smarter than bugs, I am not so sure that, when it comes to getting ourselves out of the cups we find ourselves in, we always do a better job of it. Once we are into a particular set of problems, I am not so sure all of us can think our way out of them — at least all by ourselves.

In this morning's newspaper I read an account of a farmer who killed himself. He left a wife and family behind. For most of his life he had been a successful man but now, with prices for his cattle and wheat falling, he was faced with enormous debts that he could not pay. He had inherited the farm from his father and had, we can only guess, felt that to lose the farm was to lose everything. And so, in good health and still young, he killed himself.

As I read this story, I thought of the bug in the cup. I thought of this man as stuck in a situation from which he could see no escape. And when I reread the story, it was clear to me that the farmer had not talked to his wife or his friends about being trapped in a cup. Everyone was "shocked" at his suicide. So I concluded that those who knew and loved him could only be "shocked" if he had *never* told them of how trapped he felt. And, at least from the story, it appeared to me that he had killed himself without reaching out for other possible solutions, other possible ways to get out of the cup. In a word, he had "kept his problems to himself" and died with his honor intact.

Maybe you, like me, think it is a tragedy that a man would kill himself because he could not pay a debt. Maybe you are thinking that if you had been in his shoes, you could have done something different. Sold the farm and started a business? Moved to California and become an artist? Gone back to college to become an engineer? We can only guess what he might have done with the years yet ahead of him.

But of one thing I am sure; so long as any of us take it upon only our own shoulders to solve a problem, we will be limited in how well we solve it.

Imagine with me, if you will, that we are going to take a trip to a distant planet. Our flight is booked and we are leaving next Tuesday. We have a few days to pack and the people in charge of the flight have told us we must be ready in three days. While food and water will be supplied, each of us can bring along only ten things. We will be gone from earth for one year. What would be our first step?

Should we, for example, each go home and write down the ten things we would most want to have along on such a trip and then pack them up? Or should we first have a meeting and jointly decide which *twenty* things we should take *together*?

The answer is obvious to anyone who has ever participated in this little game. In a word, you don't want to start off on a trip to a distant planet with two guitars, two television sets, and two copies of the same book. Rather, if we will work together, we will come up with a much better list, a list that doesn't overlap and one that gives each of us many more of the things we would like to take along on such a trip. My point is this: If you think that you alone must solve all the problems, then you had better be damned smart.

In my experience, people (including myself) are not nearly so smart as they sometimes think they are. We think that because our eyes and ears and brains are all in working order, that we can know what to do in all sorts of situations we have never been in before. But this simply is not true. All of us are like bugs in a cup—we can see around the insides of our cup, but we cannot see over the lip. We cannot see what lies beyond. And what we cannot see, we cannot imagine doing.

Then, too, there is the matter of information. As I have said, it is my belief that all of us make the best decisions we can—given the information we have at hand when we make the decision. For example, I have little doubt that the decision to commit suicide is the *best* decision available for people who decide to do it. They have thought everything through, weighed everything, and, when they ran all the available data through that computer in their head, suicide was *the* answer.

But wait a minute. Did they have all the information available to make the decision? Did they know, for example, that the depression they are experiencing is probably time-limited? Did they know that someone out there in the future of their lives could come to love and cherish them? Did they know that, within a few days, things could begin to change for the better and that their formula should have included these changes? Or did they, like the person in our space-trip game, just go home and pack ten things?

While I am not suggesting that suicide is always a stupid decision, I am suggesting that before we decide to kill ourselves, maybe we ought to give ourselves a bit of time to come to know something we maybe didn't know before, something that might give us a different view—maybe even a view over the edge of the cup.

So, for the next few chapters, I'm going to give you some information you may not have. This information may or may not make a difference, but I am going to bet that it will.

7 • • •

Loneliness

It would help me a great deal to know how old you are. Because if I knew how old you were, I would know better how to talk to you about what you may be going through. But since I can't know this, as best I can, I am going to talk to you as if you were any age. And, if anything, I am going to talk to you as if you were younger than I.

I am nearly fifty. Having lived this long, I know a few things about what it is like to be a boy, a teenager, a college student, a soldier, a young married person, a father, and, just now, a middle-aged man. But because I am in the middle of my life, I can't know as much about being sixty or seventy or eighty and I can't know how it is to be closer to the end of life.

Since I am closer to sixty than twenty, I cannot remember exactly what it was like to be much younger. But I won't apologize too much for where I am in my journey through life, mainly because it really won't change anything if I do.

If you are much younger than I, you might be thinking, "What can this old man say to me about loneliness that means anything?"

Or, if you are old, you might be thinking, "What can this youngster say to me that I don't already know?"

Since I am not a woman and if you are female, you can ask, "How can a man know what loneliness is like for me?"

33

To all of the above questions, I have a simple answer: I can't know your loneliness, I won't pretend to.

But because I came into this world alone, like you, and will leave it alone, like you, and because I know that all of us have had the experience of loneliness, then I think I can share with you something of what I know of loneliness. Loneliness is, when you stop to think about it, the one universal human experience. It is the one necessary condition we all share and, out of it, maybe we can come to better understand each other.

All of us are handicapped by our vital statistics. We are trapped in our age, our generation, our race, and our sex. Like it or not, we are all prisoners of our own special time and place and accidents of birth. Insofar as we are all captives of who we are, by necessity we are all limited and, in being so, are entirely alone in what we know of life. Our vision is limited, our understanding of others imperfect. In this way we are all blind and must stumble along never knowing just what life is like for another person. There can be no other way.

I can never know what it is like to be poor and black. I can never know what it is like to be raised on a reservation or called names because of the color of my skin. I can never know what it is like to be born rich and live in luxury. But although I can never know these things, it does not mean that I cannot try to understand them. Because I can never experience what another human being experiences, does not mean that I cannot appreciate him or come to feel with him about the problems of his life.

So, I would ask you this: Is there anyone anywhere who has experienced exactly what you have experienced? Is there anyone anywhere who can truly know your pain as only you know it?

I think your answer has to be no. Because that is the way it is with us humans. We know ourselves best, those close to us fairly well, and strangers not at all. But in spite of these limitations, most of us do what we can to understand one another and, so far as we are able, try to make ourselves understood.

This is why we should talk about loneliness. It is, in a way, the common bond between us. Each of us has thoughts and feelings we have kept to ourselves our whole life long. Each of us has private hopes and fears and dreams that, should even the people closest to us ask about them, we would deny. So let us talk about loneliness.

Loneliness is a killer. In its worst form, it is our enemy number one. You have known it, I have known it, everyone who ever stops to think about the meaning of one's life has known it. It is that terrible feeling that, in all the universe, there is no one who cares enough to come to us and end our aloneness. It is the one thing that hurts more than any other. It is the feeling that no one wants us, that no one really cares if we exist.

I won't kid you, loneliness is the one sure place from which thoughts of suicide can spring. It is out of loneliness that people begin to think that death may be better than life. "I couldn't be any more alone if I was dead, so why not die?" This is the terrible logic of suicide and it is born and bred in loneliness.

When you are lonely, you can look around you and see, however good or poor your vision, that others do not appear lonely. And it is this difference in what you see others have that you don't, that makes loneliness so awful.

Since I cannot know the depth of your aloneness, I may not be able to say anything that will take the sting out of whatever loneliness you may feel. But since I know that loneliness is such a terrible state, maybe it will help if I talk to you about what I believe loneliness to be and what I think you might be able to do about it.

Being Alone Versus Loneliness

In the first place, I believe there is some confusion about loneliness. To be alone is not necessarily to be lonely. You can be all alone on a mountaintop and yet not be lonely. You can live in a crowded city and be surrounded by thousands of people and yet be dying of loneliness. Or you can be a member of a family and be with people all day and night and yet, in your heart, be lonely. It is, therefore, not a matter of where you are, but how you are connected to the people around you, how you speak with them, how they hear you and how they know about you that makes the difference between being just alone and being lonely.

Many people I have worked with cannot stand to be alone. They equate being alone with loneliness. They have told me that when they are by themselves, they begin to feel empty and hollow and incomplete, as if being in the presence of others gives them meaning they do not otherwise have. They will do desperate things just for the company of others. "I go to bars every night," one young woman told me, "because I can't stand to stay home alone."

I asked her, "Are you such bad company for yourself?"

The woman stared at me. "I hadn't thought of it that way," she said. "I guess maybe I am."

As we talked more, we learned that she had never thought of herself as very interesting or funny or bright. She held a low opinion of herself and couldn't, really, see why anyone would want to spend time with her, except maybe for sex. In a word, she didn't like herself very much. And so, when she was alone, she was keeping company with someone she didn't care all that much about. And she later laughed with me that it was better to be wanted for sex, than not to be wanted at all.

But as you can see, this was a vicious cycle. She did not like casual sex, but because she needed to be with someone—anyone—to be affirmed that she was not alone, she sacrificed her self-esteem and, in the bargain, only lowered it that much more. Because, as she said, "Only a lowlife would do the things I've done."

So at least one reason for loneliness is that we don't like ourselves. I cannot, in any simple way, help you to begin to like yourself. I wish I could. But where I cannot, others can. Or maybe you can help yourself. All I know is that until you begin to like yourself, no great gains can be made against loneliness.

Until you begin to identify and know and accept that you have some value, some purpose, some good and decent qualities as a human being, you will find being alone a terrible way to spend your days.

For other lonely people, I have often recommended that they spend some time alone. I know that sounds crazy, but consider the case of the disc jockey.

Ted was a busy radio disc jockey and never failed to come on the air in a happy, cheerful voice. He had fans. He was paid well and had a girlfriend. From the outside, his life looked wonderful. But he came to me because, as he put it, "I must be crazy."

"Why are you crazy?" I asked him.

"Because despite how I appear to you, I am terribly lonely. I can't stand not to have people around me. They're like air to me. If I'm alone for just a few minutes, I begin to panic, as if I can't breathe. My girlfriend and I want to get married, but I feel I'm not ready. It's as if I need her too much. It's as if, if I married her, I would never be able to be without her. And that doesn't seem fair to her."

As I got to know Ted, I realized that he had let himself become a hollow man. Without fans and friends and people around him to tell him how clever and bright and entertaining he was, he felt empty and alone. He had, it turned out, never spent time with himself, by himself, or getting to know and like himself. Somewhere, deep in his mind, I think he thought he needed people too much and that, without them, he believed he might die of loneliness.

As goofy as it sounded to him, I suggested he walk from my office to the park across the street and sit for one hour and not talk to anyone, except maybe himself. The next time we met, he laughed and said he had failed. "Ever try to carry on a conversation with a duck?" Then he added, "That was the longest hour I ever spent. Almost painful. And ducks don't laugh at your jokes."

But the effect was good. Gradually, by spending more and more time by himself, he began to realize that he could survive without people constantly around him. He could breathe easily, think things to himself, and come to make friends with his inner thoughts and feelings. He began to feel he could make it on his own and needn't fear being alone the way he once had.

Toward the end of our sessions, I asked Ted if he could try something he had never done before, something that would give him the strength to live alone, if that should be required of him one day. The very thought of it frightened him.

"What do you suggest?" he asked.

"What do you suggest?" I said.

Ted thought a moment. "I've always wanted to take a wilderness canoe trip. Maybe I could do that."

"By yourself?"

"Is there another way?"

"I'm afraid not," I said.

And so Ted rented a canoe and drifted on a wilderness river for three days by himself. When he returned, he was beaming. He had survived aloneness and was not lonely. We ended our sessions and, within a month, Ted was married and off to a new job in another city.

The point of Ted's story is simply this: It is not being alone that is the enemy, it is the fear of being alone. And, while I do not want to make this sound too easy, it is my feeling that we all must find a way, not to endure aloneness, but to enjoy it and to grow from it.

Making Our Own Loneliness

From other people I have learned that loneliness is often of one's own making. Somewhere, somehow, we come to a belief that is wrong. We believe that other people somehow owe it to us not to let us suffer loneliness. We believe that, just because we are human beings, others will come to us to inquire after our thoughts and feelings. While this sometimes happens, I do not believe this is a good thing to count on. If anything, people tend to avoid us if we look and act lonely.

Have you ever heard yourself say, "Nobody really cares." I'm sure I have and I'm pretty sure everyone has at one time or another. It is a statement of loneliness. To say it once or twice because we feel all alone is one thing, but to believe it to be true now and forever is something else again.

In my view, a lasting belief that nobody really cares about us and, *no one can ever care about us in the future*, is the equivalent of a self-imposed death sentence. If we truly believe this is how things are today and how they will always be in the future, then what hope can there be that we can beat loneliness? None.

But let's examine this belief a bit.

Where did we get it? Is it because when we have been lonely, people have not come to us to relieve our loneliness? Have our parents been too busy and our so-called friends too preoccupied with themselves? Probably. But does that make it true forever? Or are we like little scientists with a pet theory that we are trying to prove? Have we established a hypothesis that says, "People don't care and the proof is that I am lonely and nobody is doing anything about it."

I think there is a way to test this. Let's assume for the moment that you are not the loneliest person in the world, that out there somewhere is someone who is more lonely than you. I know that is hard to believe, but stay with me.

Now let's suppose that you, being the second loneliest person in the world, decide to try to find the loneliest person in the world. How would you do this?

There is only one way. You would have to go and try to find him or her. And you would do this by reaching out to someone; asking if they had had a nice day, or did they enjoy a movie they had seen or just about any question you might think of. Since you already know you are the second loneliest person in the world, you wouldn't bother telling them this, but rather you would try to find out about them. You would ask about their feelings and thoughts and hopes and fears.

Now, what would happen?

The first thing that would happen is that you would quickly slide down to number three or four on the lonely list. And if you talked to enough people, eventually you probably wouldn't even make the list.

I know how simpleminded this sounds. But can you think of another way? I cannot. And I know that if you wait for the world to come to you to end your loneliness, you may have a very long wait indeed.

Lonely people have said to me, "But that's harder to do than you realize. I can't just go up to some stranger and start talking to them."

And I have said, "Why not?"

"Because I don't have anything to say."

"That's fine," I have said. "You don't have to say anything about yourself. In fact, you shouldn't. You already know you're the second loneliest person in the world and haven't got much going anyway. The job is to find out about them, not to tell them about yourself."

I have used this suggestion many times with many people and have never seen it fail. I have found that if lonely people will take just this one small step that, in so doing, they will learn something they didn't know. And that is that everyone is lonely to a degree and that, of all the things we like to do in this world, one of the best is to talk about ourselves. If given any opportunity at all, we can talk and talk and talk about ourselves. It is getting someone to listen that is the trick.

Once someone engages us in a conversation like this, two things generally happen: (1) we begin to like this person who encourages us to talk about ourselves, and (2) we want to know more about them and begin to ask *them* questions.

Sooner than you can imagine, a friendship is in the offing. And if loneliness is enemy number one, friendship is the FBI.

This is nothing new. Smart people have known for centuries that the quickest way to make friends and never be lonely is to ask about the other person and get him or her to talk about himself or herself. You hold back on what you would like to do (talk about yourself), while you listen and learn about someone else. It is really as simple as that.

So if you are lonely and willing to try another kind of experiment (as opposed to proving that people don't really care), then you can do something today to test this idea. You can pick out just about anybody—the person sitting next to you on the bus, the girl across the table at the lunchroom, the janitor that waxes the hall, anyone—and make a few simple inquires. "How's it going?" "It was pretty hot yesterday, wasn't it?" Or whatever it takes to get a conversation going.

Then, make it a point to learn just three things about this person; his name, where he is from, and what he does for a living or what he is studying in school. On the basis of these three things, people can begin to feel if there is a common bond possible between them. They can begin to feel the possibility of a friendship.

And the problem of getting someone to listen to us, to break into our own loneliness, will solve itself because, lo and behold, the people we have sought out will soon want to know about us. They simply can't help themselves unless, of course, they are so stuck on themselves they don't care about anyone else—in which case they probably weren't worth knowing anyway.

The key to get the ball rolling is not to talk about ourselves until asked a question and, then, to keep our answers short. Later, when we have a relationship, we can talk about ourselves much more freely. This is essentially what psychologists and psychiatrists and counselors like me do all the time—it is why people generally come to like us. Everyone likes a good listener, or so it seems.

Of course some people may look at you as if you're nuts when you start such a conversation, but that is their problem. In my experience and in the experience of the lonely people I have worked with, the fear of being rejected is only that — a fear. And if we live within the confines of our fears, then we will remain a prisoner of our loneliness and nothing will ever change.

So I think you have to ask yourself this question: Have I had any hand in my own loneliness? Have I been like the little scientist who sets out to prove that people don't really care? Have I been collecting evidence that in spite of the fact that there are five billion people on the planet, not one of them could ever be my friend?

Because if you have, then you have also been building a case for choosing death over life. And, until you (and I mean *only* you) take the first step out and away from loneliness, things will probably not change for the better.

I might take a guess as to what you're thinking right now. "Yeah, and if I try it, I'll get hurt again. I'll reach out to someone and they won't like me. It won't work."

And you might be absolutely right. It might not work. People might hurt you again. And you would have even more proof that people don't really care and that you can't ever get out of the cup.

But where, I'll ask you, does it say on your birth certificate that you have any guarantee against loneliness or that if you risk knowing and maybe loving someone that you will always come out a winner? Nowhere, that's where. I'm sorry, friend, but none of us gets guarantees that life won't be painful or that we can't get hurt.

So I'll ask you, what alternatives do we have? Can any of us just sit back and wait for someone to come to us and end our loneliness? Or do we have to take that first small step? Admittedly, it is a gamble. But like it or not, unless we want to cash in our chips and quit the game entirely, it is a gamble we all must take.

And try to remember, out there somewhere among those five billion people is someone, maybe just like you, who is about to take the same gamble. Who knows, in five billion souls, there might even be three or four or maybe even a dozen who, at this very moment, are taking the gamble. If you happen to meet up with each other, you can quarrel later over who was the loneliest.

8   • • •

The Good News
About Depression

What would you think if I told you that no matter how depressed you are today, at this very minute, that your depression is going to lift and that, sooner or later, you are going to begin to feel better? What if I told you that if you are like most depressed people, you're going to get over your depression and it will all become just a bad memory?

You'd probably say I need to have my head examined by a qualified psychologist. Well, you'd be wrong.

The good news about depression is that except for the rare case, depression is a sometime thing. The common cold of emotional problems, some four to eight million Americans are suffering from depression this very day. And, like the common cold and as miserable as they can be, most depressions eventually run their course and the person gets back to normal.

If you will take a minute to think back over your life, I think you will find that you have been sad and depressed before and gotten over it. Maybe more than once. Maybe you've never been this depressed before, but surely this isn't the first time you have felt low and down and rotten and hopeless. Unless you have been leading something of a charmed life, you've had to go through what all the rest of us have gone through from time to time—and that is the feeling of depression.

Without getting too complicated here, I want to tell you a few things about this depression business. Because I know that about sixty percent of the people who try to kill themselves are depressed when they do it, I know there is a better-than-even chance that you are depressed. And because I know you may not be an expert on depression, I'm going to try to bring you up to speed and put a little information in your head about this most-common form of emotional distress. (If you are not depressed and just angry or lonely or stressed to the maximum or feeling hopeless and helpless, you can skip ahead to those chapters and leave us occasionally depressed people to ourselves. On the other hand, if you're feeling hopeless and helpless, maybe you'd better stay with us.)

Since I've worked with hundreds of depressed people and have been there once or twice myself, I know what a chore it is to read something about depression when what I'd really like to do is go off somewhere and sleep for a couple of days or turn on the TV and let someone try to cheer me up. So, I promise to keep this short and to the point.

Being depressed is a life-threatening state of mind. Being seriously depressed is a life-threatening state of mind and body. It is the one human experience that, when it won't go away, makes us sicker and sicker until, when we are way down in the bottom of that black hole, we can't imagine ever feeling any better. I once asked a very depressed young man if he was anxious about something. "No," he sighed, "I'm too depressed to be anxious."

So I know that when you are depressed, all other feelings begin to lose their power. Nothing tastes good when you are depressed, nothing sounds good, nothing seems funny. The things that used to be worth living for lose their value. Being depressed is not caring whether you respond to life or not. And that is what depression means—failing to respond vigorously to life's demands.

When you are really depressed, it is as if nothing can be imagined ever to be good again. Not only do you feel depressed, but you begin to *think* depressed. This "stinkin' thinkin'" leads you deeper and deeper into the black hole until, finally, there doesn't seem any way out of it. Depression is, in its worst form, a kind of mental and physical paralysis.

Losses

There are lots of reasons people get depressed, more reasons than even we so-called experts think we know about. But some of the reasons are obvious and it doesn't take a genius to figure them out. We can start with losses.

Anytime we suffer a loss, we tend to get depressed. Some don't, but most of us do. If we lose a close friend, we feel the loss and we feel grief at not having that person with us. If we lose a job we wanted, we feel that too and often in the same way. If our boyfriend dumps us for another girl, that is a loss and our reaction is hurt, anger, and maybe depression. The same feeling follows losses of health, prestige, or things we wanted but find we cannot have. Even failing an important exam is a loss — a loss to our self-esteem. Anytime we suffer a loss, the chances are good we may become depressed.

But here are a couple of things to think about. Obviously, there are losses and then there are *losses*. It is one thing to lose a little finger; it is quite another thing to lose a hand — especially if you are a piano player. There are big-ticket losses and little-ticket losses and though most of us can agree that losing an arm is a big loss, we can't ever know how big a loss it is unless we are the piano player. And my point is that I can never know just how you will interpret your loss and, for that matter, neither can anyone else.

Some years ago I knew an elderly lady who had to go into a hospital for some tests and found out she was quite sick and would have to stay in the hospital for at least a month. Her husband had died the year before and the only living thing she had left in this world that meant anything to her was her cat. But they would not let the cat into the hospital. And so, when she asked her only son to see after the cat, he did what he thought was the right thing: he had it put to sleep. The lady slumped into a huge depression and stopped eating. In three days she was dead.

Now you can tell yourself that this old lady was silly, that it is stupid for anyone to die over the loss of a cat. But it doesn't matter what you think. What matters is what our lady thought about losing her cat. And that is the way it is with all of our losses — it only matters what they mean to us.

But let's look at some of the big-ticket losses, the ones we hope we will never have and yet, because life is the way it is, we may have to deal with — like it or not.

We can lose people we love. They may leave us, they may move away, they may even die. There is no getting around it, losing someone you love is going to hurt like the dickens and, unless you are made of stronger stuff than the rest of us, you are going to grieve that loss and experience what passes for depression.

We can lose our health. Until we get sick, we never understand what good health means. Most of us think we will live forever, but getting sick changes all that. Once you get good and sick or are injured and lose some major function, you can no longer pretend you are made of stainless steel. Physical pain that goes on and on is, by the way, a major cause of depression and almost no one who has suffered pain for any length of time can avoid becoming depressed.

We can lose our money. You might not think that losing money could lead to depression, but it does. Money, in our society, equals personal power, and personal power equals control over our own lives. When we lose a lot of money, or maybe all we have, we lose the power to control what happens to us. And when we lose control over what can happen to us, the loss can be unbearable and lead to depression.

These are examples of big-ticket losses and there are many more. Sometimes people suffer more than one major loss in a short period of time and, as sure as the clouds of depression begin to gather, there will follow a long dark storm.

Maybe you are wondering . . . if these kinds of losses can lead to depression, so what? So this: What if you've had a very bad year? What if, as you run down the list of things we may all have to lose someday, you've found yourself saying, "Yes, I lost that." And, "Yes, I lost that, too." What if, as years go in your life, you've had an unusually rotten one? Maybe the worst one you will ever have.

Then please consider this. What if, as rotten as this last year has been, it is the worst one you will ever have? What if they couldn't possibly line up one like it again? Then, even though you are depressed now, can you imagine ever being this depressed again? Let's hope not.

So, assuming you are depressed, maybe you deserve to be. Maybe anyone in exactly your same position would be depressed. Your depression could very well be a *normal* reaction to the losses you've suffered. So maybe you are not so different as you think you are. Because if you think you have a corner on depression, you couldn't be more wrong. Remember I said that as of this morning, there might be as many as eight million of your fellow countrymen out there suffering the same symptoms. The depressed crowd is a big one.

Because everyone loses something sometime, depression is going around like a bad virus and anyone who isn't depressed today certainly has been at one time or another, or is likely to be at some time in the future. None of us can get off and on the planet and entirely avoid getting depressed a few times—unless, of course, we have figured out how to get through life without feeling the pain of losing something dear to us.

So, if you have suffered some terrible loss or losses, it is true I cannot know what they are or just how, exactly, you will take them. But I know this: You are no different from the rest of us. If cut, you will bleed. If hurt, you will feel pain. If you lose greatly, you will grieve. If you lose something very important to you, you

know about our anger; its source, what it does to us and how it affects the way we think and feel.

Maybe you have never thought of yourself as an angry person. Maybe you can say, "I never get mad." But my guess is that if you can say this of yourself, you may not be in touch with what is troubling you. It is even possible that you may not even know what is making you angry. Or, if you do know, you may be ignoring or minimizing or playing down those obstacles and roadblocks or people that stand between you and your dreams. Since we learn how to express our anger at an early age, maybe it was not okay to get mad in your family.

Over the years I have met many people who said, "We were not permitted to lose our temper at home. It just wasn't allowed." If this was your situation as a child, then maybe you are out of touch with your anger. Like many others, maybe you do not even realize how angry you are. And, since suicide is often an angry act generated out of frustration and burning resentment, it is, I think, important that you come to grips with the possibility that you may be mad enough to kill yourself.

Ask yourself this: "Is any part of my wish to die because I am frustrated with the way things are going?" If your answer is yes, then you may be more angry than you think. So let's talk about anger.

Of all the emotions, anger is maybe the least complicated. It is part of our biological makeup and a necessary part of living. Unless everything goes smoothly for you every single day and you never break so much as a shoelace, then you must experience frustration. And if you experience frustration, then you must experience anger — even though you may call it something else.

Here's what happens inside us when we become frustrated and begin to feel anger: our heart beats faster, our blood pressure rises, sugar is released into our blood stream, our muscles tense, and our bodies get ready for physical combat. Biologically, we are preparing to deal with some pain or threat or fear and, though we may try to stop a rush of anger, there isn't really much we can do to override the reaction. Or at least it seems that way.

I have met many people who do not even know when they are angry. They say they are "upset." Or they say they are "down." Or they say they would just as soon be left alone. Even though they are experiencing a strong emotion (and you can see it by the way the veins in their necks bulge or their faces turn red or they clench their fists or jaws), they will smile and say, "No, of course I'm not angry. I'm just fine." They may be denying their anger or simply don't know what to call it. It doesn't matter much for our purposes right now, except to illustrate that many angry people don't know what's going on inside them or, if they do, they attempt to deny the feeling.

How you come to know your anger has a lot to do with the way you were raised. In some families, expressions of anger are simply not permitted. In others, anger is not only permitted, but encouraged. In families where anger is understood as natural and, therefore, accepted and channeled into healthy communication, anger is not an enemy. But where children are raised to fear their anger as if it were some kind of raging beast that, once released, would run amok and kill everything in sight, anger can become an enemy. To experience anger in such a family is to be taught that your angry feelings don't exist or, if they do, something must be wrong with you.

Over the years I have met many people who thought feeling angry was the same thing as *being* crazy. And, when they were extremely angry, they often felt they were about to lose control and maybe do something terrible and awful. Not infrequently, what they thought to do was to hurt themselves.

Anger in Our Culture

If you look to our society for guidance about the meaning of anger and how it should be expressed, things suddenly get very confused. It is okay for a football player to get angry in a game and try to "kill" the guy on the other team. It is not okay for the fans to do this to the visiting fans. It is okay for our heroes on TV to punch, gouge, knife, and shoot just about anyone who deserves it; it is not okay for those of us watching the show to do this to equally deserving bad guys we know. Our government preaches peace, but if we get angry enough we launch retaliatory "air strikes" and drop huge bombs on those who are frustrating us. You might even say that we, as a country, teach peace but practice vengeance.

For what it is worth, I think there is something crazy going on here. What I think is crazy is that many of us are convinced that once we become angry we have to do something aggressive. We say we hate violence, but we love it in our sports, our movies, and our TV shows. We believe that once we are angry enough, we are justified in doing something destructive. If someone makes us mad enough, we seem to take the position that, "Okay, now you've done it. You'd better watch out!"

Our religious leaders try to talk us out of our frustration→ anger→aggression habits but, just between you and me, I think they've got their hands full. It seems that hardly anyone "turns the other cheek" these days.

So what, you are probably asking, has all this to do with thinking about suicide?

Let's suppose for the moment that you, like many others, do not know your own anger very well—how it feels, where it comes from, and what to do with it when you feel it. Let's suppose that when a rush of anger comes over you, you begin to get more and more upset until, at the peak of it, you feel like you are going out of control. You are mad as hell about something and, before this fit of anger is finished, someone or something is going to pay.

But who should pay? The person you're mad at? No, you can't punch a teacher, the boss, a husband or wife or a brother or a sister. Hit a friend and you buy loneliness. Besides, we're not supposed to strike out at others. So, all dressed up with no place to go, what will become of your anger? Where does it go? If anger *always* leads to aggression, how can anger ever be your friend?

I personally don't think raw, pure, unadulterated anger can ever be anyone's friend. Runaway anger is always an enemy. Anger with no place to go can lead to suicide.

So what can you do?

You can do what Charlie, a client of mine, used to do when he became uncontrollably angry. "I just double up my fist and punch the wall," he said.

"How often do you do that?" I asked.

"A couple of times a week," he said. "It's better than hitting people. Besides, it's plasterboard and most times my fist goes right through. But sometimes I hit a stud."

Charlie had broken the bones in his hands so many times he'd lost track, and he laughed when I said it was a good thing he didn't live in a brick house. Anger was not Charlie's friend.

Or you can learn the art of cutting people down with sarcasm. You can learn to say mean and nasty things to people to make them feel bad. Verbal aggression, though physically less harmful, is still harmful and, if you use it, you will end up short of friends and not liking yourself very much. Of all the things people do to hurt each other, sarcasm leaves the deepest scars. And, again, anger is not your friend.

Or you can hold all your anger in until, one day, you may develop high blood pressure or headaches or ulcers or some other illness that the researchers say may be the result of constant tension built up by unspent anger. Working slowly over time, such anger may one day make you sick.

But the worst way in which anger is our enemy is when we turn it on ourselves, when we become so frustrated in our desire to get back at someone that, finding no one else to hurt, we start looking in the mirror for a victim. This is why, even though I do not like the term, suicide is sometimes referred to as self-murder — the assumption being that the suicide was an act of destruction directed at the self.

Options for Anger

Now let me suggest something to you. What if I told you that just because you're angry, you don't have the right to go around breaking things or calling people names or hitting them or, for that matter, hurting yourself? What if I told you that just because you are mad as hell, it doesn't mean you automatically, like some robot, have to blow your stack and lose control of yourself? What if I told you that, no matter what you've read or heard about how good it is to "get your anger out" that, in fact, letting your anger out was the most stupid thing you could do? And especially if you kill yourself in the process?

Well, I'm saying all of that. Despite what was once believed about anger, research is showing that once you explode and lose control of your anger, you are more likely to do it again. Research is showing that the way we express our anger is a learned habit, just as we learn to read or ride a bike. And if you learned how to express your anger in ways that make anger your enemy then, as I see it, you can unlearn the old ways and learn new ones.

I can hear you thinking, "Ho. Ho. Ho. He doesn't know *my* anger. My anger is different!"

If you were sitting in my office right now and said this, you would have an argument on your hands. I would argue that since you are from the same galaxy, the same planet, and the same species, that you are no different in the anger department from me or from anyone else. You learned how to express and handle your anger just the way the rest of us learned how to express and handle our anger. The lesson may have been different, but the process was the same. And, since you've a large and generally useful brain perched up there on your shoulders, you can probably do something intelligent about your anger. You can learn to handle it differently, maybe learn to manage it in useful and productive ways.

If you are willing to accept the idea that the way in which you express your anger is *not* automatic and out of your control, then I think there is a good chance you can change. You can turn an enemy into a friend. I can't do this for you in a book like this, but I know professional help is available. In some cities agencies even offer what are called "Anger Management" workshops. And there are several good self-help books on the subject. The point is, you don't have to go on being stuck in the frustration → anger → aggression formula.

The basics of learning to know and use your anger well are as follows:

(1) Learn to identify your anger quickly. If you feel a sudden bit of tension, or a flush come to your face or you find yourself clenching your jaws or thinking, "Damn, that makes me mad!" then say to yourself, "Ah ha! This is the first sign of anger. I know you."

(2) Next, say to yourself, THINK! When we are angry, we tend to switch our brains off and let our glands run the show. Given where anger can sometimes go, this is just plain stupid. When you have a runaway freight train, you don't tell the engineer to kindly leave the train. No, you ask him to stay on board and try to get the brakes working. Thinking is to anger what brakes are to a runaway train.

(3) Then, ask yourself why you are feeling angry. Try to identify just who or what is making you bristle. Ask yourself: Am I frightened? Am I threatened? Has someone just said something to hurt me? How am I being frustrated? Answers to these questions will help you enormously because you will at least begin to understand whence your anger arises. And it will lead you to the next question.

(4) What is it I want and what will I do with all this power? Anger is a powerful emotion and, when you are feeling it, you are feeling strong. What, you should ask, can I do with all this power and strength? How can I direct it to benefit me and those around me?

Admittedly, this is the tough part of knowing how to use our anger and requires the greatest creativity. Pretending that nothing is wrong, or exploding, or turning the anger inward and against yourself produces nothing and benefits no one—least of all the angry person. What we need when we become angry is to set a goal, something to shoot for. We need to know what is making us angry and what, in the short and the long run, we want to change.

When you have identified that you are angry, know who or what it is that is making you feel that way, and have instructed yourself to THINK, then that is exactly what you should do. Step back, count to ten, and start to think. Thinking while angry is difficult, but not impossible. And some wonderful things begin to happen when angry people start to think instead of going on being angry.

Remember, it was because of his anger over racial discrimination that Martin Luther King Jr. thought to change a nation and, maybe one day, a world. Martin Luther King Jr. did not lose his temper. No, he knew his anger, knew the face of it, and the source of it and knew that aggression and violence need not automatically follow from anger. He did not strike others. He did not burn things. He did not get sick and die from his anger. And he did not turn it on himself. No, Martin Luther King Jr. put anger to work for a great good. And, in so doing, his was a wonderful anger.

It is a sad irony that a man who could not manage his own anger assassinated one of the greatest men who could.

But back to you. Since your anger is as natural as your breathing, you might as well get to know it. You might as well just walk up and shake hands. Anger is a great source of power and a great teacher of what we like and don't like in this world. From our anger we can grow. From our anger we can set goals and do good things for ourselves and others. Once we have come to know and master our anger we can have a strong and trustworthy friend. We do not need to be anger's slaves.

Most importantly, we need never be its victims.

So, if we can come to know and name our anger and learn who or what it is that is making us feel this powerful emotion, we need not be frightened by it and we need not be controlled by it. Rather, we can stop, think, set a goal, and plan a move that will change our situation for the better.

Please remember: To be angry is natural. To be angry at ourselves and others is normal. But to be so angry at another that you turn this awesome aggressive power on yourself is neither natural nor normal. It is, rather, an expression of the formula that frustration leads to anger leads to aggression. And, if you are not careful and smarter than the average bear, you may become a victim of it.

So before you kill yourself to "show" someone just how mad you are at them, consider that, should you succeed, your suicide will have created nothing, contributed nothing, and changed nothing. True, you will have made a statement about how angry you were, but ask yourself, "Do I have to say it this way?"

I hope not.

10 _____ ...

Maximum Stress

I want to begin this chapter with a story. And I want to end it with a story. In between, I want to share with you a few things about stress. I know that stress is so much written and talked about these days that the subject has become stressful itself. But I hope that if you have been experiencing a lot of whatever stress is lately (and this experience has led to thoughts of suicide), then maybe you will find something of value in the next few pages.

Amy was twenty-one and beautiful. She had married her high-school sweetheart one year ago. Her husband, an engineer, had taken a job in the city where I work, a job that required Amy to move from her home in Utah. The move had been difficult and Amy had to leave many important things behind—her apartment, her job, her best girlfriend, her mother, her home town.

Shortly after the move, Amy learned she was pregnant. She was happy, her husband was not. Chuck did not want children just now and was angry with Amy for not preventing the pregnancy. They had assumed a big mortgage on their new home and he did not feel they could afford to start a family. Chuck began to stay out late and Amy suspected he was having an affair. He refused to see a marriage counselor when Amy suggested they needed to.

Sensing she must begin to take care of herself, Amy started

looking for work. Confused and distracted by what was happening in her marriage, she was driving to a job interview when she ran a red light. Her car was struck broadside and Amy suffered a broken collarbone and a painful neck injury. The baby was fine, but she would have to be very careful during the rest of her pregnancy. It was then her sister called to say their mother had not been feeling well. The diagnosis, confirmed a week later, was terminal cancer.

When Amy broke the news of her mother's illness and that she wanted to return to Utah to be with her, Chuck said, "Fine. You can stay there. I want a divorce, anyway."

Alone, desperate, depressed, in physical pain, and pregnant, Amy slashed her wrists. It was then that she came to see me.

I won't detail how Amy finally worked things out, but she did and she survived. Amy had always been a strong person and, once the storm had passed and the hard decisions had been made, she was able to right herself and get back on track with her life. And she is doing very well now.

The point of Amy's story is this: While into every life a little rain must fall, sometimes you get a hurricane.

One Way to Think about Stress

As I cannot know what stress you have been under lately, I can only guess that maybe your story is similar to Amy's. Or maybe it is worse. Or, maybe, the stress in your life has not been coming in large doses, but is rather an ever-present strain that is slowly grinding you down. I will try to cover both kinds of stress.

First, there is nothing bad about stress. It is not evil. It is not toxic. Stress just is. It is everywhere and none of us escapes it. Without some stress, we could not achieve our potential. Without some stress, we would never be challenged to try our best and to learn of what stuff we are made. A little stress, the experts say, is good for us.

But there are also times when the stress we are under exceeds

our capacity to manage it. And, assuming you have been thinking about the suicide decision, I am going to further assume you
are dealing with what I have chosen to call maximum stress. And
maximum stress is, simply put, that amount of stress that you
(and you alone) feel is intolerable.

When it comes to measuring stress, it doesn't matter one bit
what others think is or is not stressful. What matters is what *you*
think is stressful. If you think public speaking is stressful, it is. If
you think taking an exam is stressful, it is. If you think asking a
girl for a date is stressful, it is. You and only you can define what
is stressful, and you do this by reading what your own body
says — what your stomach says, what your heartbeat says, what
your sweat glands say. The body cannot but respond to what
your mind perceives as stress. Called the "fight or flight" response, your autonomic nervous system goes into action when
you are faced with what appears to you to be dangerous or
possibly harmful to you.

Most of us know this kind of body response to acute stress.
And, if we are smart, we pay attention to it. We may use it to get
"up" for some competition or other challenge or, if it persists and
interferes with our ability to function, we find ways to avoid it.
We change jobs or relationships that we feel are unduly stressful.
And, sometimes, we avoid stress we shouldn't. But, in any event,
most of us know the physiological side of stress and know when
our body is ready for flight or fight.

But not all signs of stress are so obvious to us. Or, as is often the
case, we are unaware of what is causing stress in our lives. And it
is this lack of knowledge about what is causing us stress that is the
most dangerous to us. Because when we do not know what is
causing us stress, there isn't much we can do to combat it.

In terms of what I have chosen to call maximum stress and the
kinds of life events that often lead people to think of suicide, I
think it would be helpful to think of stress as change. (This not a
new way to think about stress, as researchers have been working
on this idea for a couple of decades.)

Consider for the moment that change, any change, requires us to adjust to that change. Once something changes in our lives, we can't go on the way we always have. Rather, we must make some kind of adjustment to what is new in our lives. This takes energy. And, according to the theory, if we have to adjust to too many changes in too short a period of time, we may begin to experience excessive stress.

If you think of life changes as stressful events and accept for the moment that the effects of stress can add up, then what will happen to you if you are required to adjust to a great many changes over a short period of time? Might you, at some point, reach or exceed your ability to handle the accumulated stress? Might you, like Amy, begin to feel overwhelmed by stress and seek some way out of what appears to be an impossibly stressful situation?

Here is a brief summary of Amy's change/stress factors:

(1) Marriage.

(2) Move from comfort of own apartment.

(3) Move away from her friends and family and sources of support.

(4) Loss of her job when she moved.

(5) Assumption of a large debt (the new home).

(6) Learning she was pregnant.

(7) Negative changes in her marriage.

(8) Injured in automobile accident (loss of physical health and sense of well being).

(9) Anticipated loss of her mother through terminal illness.

(10) Separation and divorce and the associated loss of self-esteem and sense of self-worth.

No matter how you slice it, Amy was not having a good year. Ten major changes, ten major realities to adjust to. It isn't difficult to see that if you add up all the changes in Amy's life over the past year that she had, even though she had always been a strong person, exceeded her threshold for adaptation to stress—which is why, according to Amy, she made a suicidal gesture.

"I couldn't take it anymore," she said. "It was just too much."

In talking with me, Amy agreed that it would be pretty impossible to have another year in her life quite as stressful as the one she had just been through. And, by giving herself the benefit of the long view of her life, she was able to see that the odds against a similar series of events were nearly impossible. And so, soon enough, she began to feel her old strength return and she began to cope for the better. Her thoughts of suicide diminished quickly and, as Amy said toward the end of our sessions, "I wouldn't dream of killing myself now."

Amy's life is not so different from the rest of ours. We are, all of us, bound to have bad years, years of maximum stress. The trick, as I see it, is to know this year is coming and to greet it with a kind of grim determination to make it through. And if we can do this maybe we can, like Amy, be the stronger for having made it through and, even if we are broken, our healing will make us stronger.

Sudden Overloads

I have, pinned on a corkboard over my desk at work, a little piece of wisdom that came to me one day when I was dealing with some major changes in my life. That little wisdom reads: "The only thing worse than change, is *sudden* change."

I keep this little note stuck to the message board above my desk to remind myself that even though I know I can handle a fair number of changes in my life, the day may come when things are happening so fast I'll need to remember this basic rule about stress. And that rule is this: If change is stressful, sudden change can be catastrophic.

If you, at this moment, are caught up in sudden and catastrophic changes in your life, major losses or reversals or setbacks from which you can anticipate no relief, then you may be undergoing a sudden overload of stress. And, if you are, then maybe it will help to know that certain things are likely to be going on inside you—things which, if you understand them, may help you to control, if not the events themselves, at least your reaction to them.

First, I think that there are times in our lives when certain events can throw us into a tailspin. Sudden changes entirely beyond our span of control sweep over us like a tornado and there is nothing, but nothing, we can do to alter their course. The stock market may crash and, with it, our life savings. Our employer may go bankrupt and we are suddenly thrown out of work. Someone we thought loved us suddenly announces he or she is leaving us for someone else. Without warning our lives are turned upside down and backwards and we are, like a person swept up into the funnel of a tornado, sent tumbling, tossed and turned and every which way but loose.

It is, during these sudden overloads of stress, that we begin to grasp at solutions, at any solution that will give us some relief from our present circumstance. We need to regain some sense of control over what is happening. And it is then that the idea of suicide seems better than our present turmoil and sense of despair. At least with suicide, we can know the outcome, we can get control of what is going to happen next.

But I want you to think about something for a moment. What if, despite how impossible things may seem right now and how guilty or angry or depressed you may feel, you are, in fact, *not* in control of these events. What if, instead, certain things are just going to happen and neither you nor anyone else can do anything to stop them? What if, rather, you are simply going to have to ride this one out and let things happen the way they are going to happen?

The people in Alcoholic's Anonymous have a wonderful prayer that helps them stay sane and sober. Called the Serenity Prayer, it reads: "God grant me the serenity to accept the things I cannot change, courage to change the things I can, and the wisdom to know the difference."

Of all the phrases by which people live their lives, I can think of none that contains more good sense than this one. Because, within it, is the notion that there are things that happen to us in this life that, despite however much we would wish them different, they will not be different. And that we, if we are to survive, must come to accept those things as they are and to do so with grace and dignity.

So, if by chance you are undergoing a sudden overload of stress and are feeling confused and disoriented as to your purpose, your values, your beliefs, and your traditions, then maybe it is time to stand firm in the eye of the storm and accept that which you cannot change. Because from such a stance, you may find that which you seek — a sense of serenity and peace.

Up or Out?

Because of the way the world seems to be going these days, I want to say a couple of words about life in these times and the stress with which we must all learn to cope.

We are, every one of us, required to change and adapt constantly. Some of the futurists say that the world will continue to change; our values, our ideas, our technology, where we live, the jobs we do, the people we know. And, the futurists say, these constant changes will take place rapidly, more rapidly than ever before in the history of the world. What is steady and sure and right side up today, will be shaky and upside down tomorrow. And while we may not like this constant change, this underlying sense of insecurity, it isn't like there is much any of us can do about it. You can't stop the future, and you can't stop change.

So what must we do? My own personal feeling is that since we cannot greatly reduce many of the sources of stress and the requirements for change made of us, we must, then, come to a different and more healthy perspective on what it means to live in these times. We must, by thinking differently about our lives, come to know that we will all undergo changes; little changes, big changes, constant changes. And we must learn to grow in such a way as to be ready for change, yes, even learn to look forward to it.

But to do this, I think we need to examine something I feel is pretty crazy in our society right now. And that craziness has to do with the stress and pressures we put upon ourselves as a result of thinking there is only one path to happiness and satisfaction. The direction of that narrow path is up.

By "up" I mean that many of us look at our lives as requiring that we always be moving in a direction that takes us from wherever we are now to some new, more successful, and higher place. We are a B student now, we should become an A student. We play high-school basketball, but we should be shooting for a college scholarship. We are a college player, but we will not have fulfilled our mission until we play for the National Basketball Association. We have a job we like as a skilled craftsman, but we must move up to that of a supervisor. We like being a mother and a housewife, but we are not fulfilling ourselves if we do not go back to school to start a career so we can move up.

Up. Up. Up. Everywhere I look in my counseling work, I see troubled people dissatisfied with themselves. I see people dissatisfied with themselves because they are not moving up. Or, if they are moving up, they are not moving up fast enough. They, themselves, may be satisfied with their jobs or schoolwork, but their spouses or parents or friends feel they should be moving up. College students fret and worry about their grades because, as sure as there is a life after college, they won't move you up the corporate ladder if you don't have excellent marks. Up. Up. Up. The only path is up.

And this is not the end of it. More and more these days I work with men and women whose lives, by any reasonable standard, are entirely successful. They have cars and microwaves and video recorders and good health and friends and they have accomplished what every American one day hopes to accomplish— arrival. They have arrived and taken the American dream in both hands. But guess what? They are not happy. Why? Because now that they are up, there is no place left to go. I had one successful lawyer tell me, "I wish I could start over, back at the beginning."

"Why?" I asked him.

"Because then I could start moving up again."

What was interesting about this man was that, at the peak of his career, at the peak of his powers as an attorney, at a time when his personal and family life were going perfectly and he was making more money than he ever dreamed was possible, he was thinking about suicide.

Why? Because, as I came to know Jim and his view of life, he had run the course of moving *up* to its logical end. He had arrived, and now that he was there, he had nothing more to do, nothing more to look forward to, nothing more to dream for, plan for, work for. He had, simply put, lived out his life until his dreams were spent. And now he was bankrupt and wanted out.

And where did Jim want to go? Just out. Suicide seemed a logical destination.

I have sometimes wondered if our obsession with always moving up doesn't set the stage for depression and suicidal thinking, both on the way and once we get wherever it was we thought we were going. The game of always moving up doesn't permit us to stop and smell the roses. We haven't time. We're too busy. Because we need to be moving up, we feel guilty if we stop to feel good about our accomplishments. It is as if we can never be satisfied because, in our drive to get someplace else, we can take no joy in where we are. Too many people, at least in my view, live to work rather than work to live.

And fewer and fewer people know how to play. Play is for kids. In my work, I see dozens of grown, mature people who, at the end of their work careers, are suddenly adrift. They don't know how to play. They don't know what to do with themselves now that they no longer work. Life has no meaning for them. They get depressed. And when they get depressed because life has no meaning, they start thinking suicide. As one man told me, "If I can't work, I might as well be dead."

The second part of this craziness of up and out, then, has to do with getting out. If you can't move up, then you'd better move out. The military works this way at the higher echelons of the officer corps. If you are not moving up in some corporations, then you must be stagnant and not contributing. And so, if you don't get moving up, you'd better move out.

You see it in young people who are told that if they don't get going on their studies, they won't make it into college. And if they don't make it into college, they won't make it into a good job where they can start moving up. And so, if they don't get going on their grades, they might as well get out. Many young people do just that—and "out" means the suicide decision.

Japan, a country that pushes its young students to the breaking point generation after generation, has a horrendous suicide rate around the time of the national exams—the exams that determine whether or not you will even have the opportunity to move up.

This up-or-out philosophy, at least in my opinion, is nothing short of insane. It does not permit people to be happy being average. It does not permit people to be comfortable doing a job they like. It does not permit someone to get a C in a history class and still feel as if he or she has learned something worthwhile. It doesn't allow us to take a little time to relax and enjoy what we have already done. Rather, the up-and-out philosophy drives us farther and farther and faster and faster until we become victims of our own relentless chase to be someplace else. And, though we complain of the stress, we don't seem to understand that it is stress of our own making.

If, by chance, you have bought this up-or-out philosophy of life, then what will happen to you if you hit a major and unexpected life stress? What if, out of the blue, you are the victim of some unforeseen tragedy? A promising athlete, you are badly injured and can no longer pursue your sport. An up-and-coming business executive, you are fired when the new management takes over. The man of your dreams whom you are about to marry dies in an automobile accident. The farm you inherited from your father is lost in a bankruptcy.

These things happen. They happen to people we know and they happen to us. And when they do, they amount to a dose of maximum stress. But are they things that signal the end of our lives? If we can no longer move up, must we move out? Is our path through life so narrow? Or, maybe, does our path fork around the next bend?

I ask you these questions because it is my strong feeling that too many of us see only one way to make it in the world. We see our future tied too tightly to our past and our present. However we come to believe it, we believe that we *must* succeed in whatever we set out to do and that not to succeed is to fail—and I mean to fail utterly.

This either-or, black-or-white, win-or-lose thinking is a dangerous place to be when we are hit with some kind of major life change. Because, if we are trapped into thinking we can live only one way, or with only one person, or by doing only one kind of work, and that we must always be moving up, then we lack what every creature that has ever survived on this planet has—and that is adaptability. If we cannot roll with the punches, then even the little punches can put us down.

And so, if you have been under some kind of maximum stress that is requiring you to make major changes in your life and, as a result, you are feeling that you cannot make these changes, then maybe you are trapped in that up-or-out philosophy. Maybe, in thinking about the "out" part of it, you are thinking that at least by committing suicide you will be getting out from under the stress.

If this is true, then I want you to consider something. I want you to consider that despite how traumatic the stress in your life has been lately, it is at least possible that *how* you are seeing this stress and how you are reacting to it has something to do with your philosophy of life. When bad things happen to us (and they are bound to), we must interpret them. And how we interpret them is part of our philosophy of life.

In the last chapter of this book, I have taken the liberty of asking you to think about your philosophy of life. I don't ask that you share my philosophy about how one gets along in this world, only that it might help to examine your own philosophy and, if you haven't done so lately, give it a once-over. I ask you do this because, though we may not be able to change the world, there is one thing we can change—and that is the way we think about it and what we do with our lives while we have them.

So, I will ask again: Is what is happening to you really the end? Or is it a crisis that will pass and, coming on its heels, will there be some new opportunity, something you never dreamed possible? Finally, I hope that if you have inadvertently bought the up-or-out philosophy of how one is supposed to live one's life and all that that entails, then maybe you, like me, feel this is not a healthy way to think—and especially if it has led you to thoughts of self-destruction.

At the beginning, I said that I would end this chapter with a story. This is a story I heard from a friend of mine and I do not know its origin. Therefore, I will apologize beforehand if the author is offended at my borrowing it.

The story is of an old peasant man named Ivan who, though poor in material things, is rich in wisdom. He lives on a small farm with his wife and only son. His wealth, such as it is, is in the form of a single, but fine, stallion.

One day in the early spring, the stallion breaks its tether rope and runs away into the mountains. Upon hearing of this news, Ivan's friend and neighbor comes to call.

"Oh, Ivan!" his friend cried. "I heard your horse has run away. Now you have nothing. All your wealth is gone. What will you do now that you are even poorer than before? How terrible it is!"

"Maybe," said Ivan. "It is too soon to tell."

Then, two days later, the stallion returned. And with him were five mares.

"Oh, you lucky man," said Ivan's friend, filled with envy.

"Now you are rich. Now you have six horses. What good luck! What good fortune!"

"Maybe," said Ivan. "We will see. . . ."

When the mares had been caught and corralled, Ivan's son set out to break them to saddle and plow. But in mounting the first mare, he was thrown by the wild horse against the fence and his leg was badly broken.

"Ahhh," cried Ivan's friend on learning of the accident. "Your luck is bad after all. This is terrible! This is awful! Your only son has a broken leg! Who will help you with your planting and your harvest? I feel sorry for you, Ivan. I have two healthy sons to help me and now I feel I am the lucky one and you are the unfortunate one. Such bad tidings!"

"Maybe," said Ivan.

Then, in the week that followed, the king's soldiers came to the village to take all the healthy young men off to fight the king's new war. Ivan's son was spared.

I hope the reason I tell this story is clear. I hope that what is in this story for us all is that, no matter how terrible and awful things may seem today, something quite unexpected can happen tomorrow. And, if we will but wait the bad times out, things just might get better.

In the end, I think the good life lived is not one without tragedy, but one in which the tragedies were endured and risen above. Because, as sure as I know anything, the view backward from our own future will teach us that today's miseries are tomorrow's memories — some sad, some sweet, some even comic — and that what we have to do, then, is hang in there. By our fingernails if necessary.

11   ···

Too Hopeless to Hope

In many fields of medicine just now researchers are looking for what are called "magic bullets." A magic bullet is a drug that specifically attacks and destroys the disease-causing agent or virus or process that is threatening the patient's life. Unfortunately, modern psychiatry and psychology have few magic bullets. But, if those of us in the helping professions could pick one from among all the magic bullets that might one day be found, you can bet we would all pray the first one they find is the one that destroys hopelessness.

Whatever other emotions you may be feeling now—depression, anger, loneliness, or a terrible sense of loss—none would worry me more than if you are feeling your situation is hopeless. And the reason for my concern is that despite whatever other emotional state you may be in, the state of hopelessness is the most dangerous one. Because to be without hope is to be despairing of *any* future, of *any* relief, *any* cure, and of *any* promise that things will ever change for the better. And it is from this frame of mind, this sense of utter discouragement, that thoughts of suicide grow strong and robust and take on the shape of an acceptable, if final, solution.

So if you are feeling too hopeless to hope, I won't kid you, I am worried for you. And although I have no magic bullet for your hopelessness, I want to share with you what I know of hopelessness, where it comes from, and what you might do to put an end to it.

As I have told many clients over the years, I wish I could give them an injection of hope or a handful of hope pills or direct them to a book to read that would give them that priceless relief from their sense of despair. And I wish whatever I might do for them would work in minutes, not days or weeks or months. (Such are the fantasies of therapists.) But, unfortunately, the passing of hope from one person to another is not so easy. It takes time and losses and failures and repeated defeats to fall into the hole of hopelessness and, in turn, it takes time and winning and successes to climb out again. But it can be done. It is done.

As a professional psychologist, I cannot ethically recommend a specific religious solution to hopelessness. But I am sure that, for some, this is the solution. And if finding a way to your God is what you need, then I strongly encourage you to begin that journey. And to begin it now.

Where Does Hopelessness Come From?

One thing I want you to know about hopelessness is that you do not have to be depressed to feel hopeless. Many, if not most, depressed people experience some degree of hopelessness. But hopelessness can overtake any of us. And hopelessness, research has shown, is the one common thread among the majority of those who elect the suicide option. Despairing of any future or solution to their problems, the utterly hopeless frequently find themselves thinking, "What's the use? I might as well be dead."

To help you understand hopelessness, I will rely on the work of several psychologists whose ideas and research have done much to shed light on this most vexing state of mind. Martin Seligman, Aaron Beck, and many others have been working to understand a concept they call "learned helplessness." Learned helplessness means just what it says; that people, by experiencing repeated failures when they try to change their world, eventually learn that no matter what they try to do, they are helpless to control events in their lives. And, once they feel they are helpless to control their own futures, they fall quickly into a state of depression and the associated frame of mind called hopelessness.

Here, in a nutshell, is how learned helplessness occurs. Excluding those people whose depressions may be biological in nature, the great majority of those of us who become depressed or dispirited become so in response to the loss of a loved one, or because of our failure to succeed in work or school, or through financial setbacks or because, for whatever reason, we come to believe that no matter how hard we try, our trying doesn't matter. Even successful people can come to believe that it isn't how hard you try, but the lucky breaks you get that make the difference in the happiness equation.

This feeling that whatever you do doesn't matter is at the heart of learned helplessness. It is as if, after you have been clobbered again and again by life, you come to believe that bad things *just happen* to you and there is *nothing* you can do to prevent them from happening. And, once you have arrived in this strange world where your efforts to change or control it don't matter, it is a short step to a sense of hopelessness.

Sheila, a depressed young woman I had worked with for several weeks, summed up her state of helplessness and hopelessness in a few short sentences. "It's as if I am cursed," she said. "I tried to talk to my boyfriend about our problem. But he wouldn't listen. I've interviewed for a dozen jobs, but nobody will hire me. I go on a diet and gain weight. The other day I stumbled and broke a bone in my ankle. Now I can't even look for work. It seems like the harder I try, the more I fail. It's hopeless, that's what it is."

Sheila, though she didn't know it, fitted the pattern of learned helplessness perfectly. She had been trying to get her life together, but nothing was working. And, after several months of trying, she had come to the conclusion that no matter what she did, she was going to fail. Then, to try to minimize her sense of failure and contain the losses to her self-esteem, she began to predict that she would fail even before she tried. "Now," she said, "when I go to a job interview, I know they're not going to hire me. I know it before I go into their office and I can see it immediately in their faces. And, you know, I think they can see it in my face, too."

Sheila was right. After experiencing a long string of failures, it becomes easier and easier to predict your own future. The safest prediction, given your own history, is to predict that you will fail again. And, once you begin to predict your own failures, you won't be disappointed because, though you may not be aware of it, you will begin to do things to ensure those failures. As Sheila said, "Even before he might have offered me the job, I told the last employer I interviewed with that I would understand if he didn't have anything for me. I guess I helped make up his mind for him. Stupid, huh?"

What Sheila did may have been stupid, but it made sense for her. By anticipating a rejection, she cushioned her next fall. But this is the psychology of learned helplessness and, to be more blunt about it, the psychology of the loser.

Sheila was not a loser. She had been a successful high-school student, earning honors in debate. She had worked her own way through two years of business school and done very well. She had learned to play the guitar on her own. She had helped her mother get back on her feet after her father had died. She had, in a word, done a great many things that, from an objective point of view, could be termed successes. But, and here is the key, she had not done anything she thought of as successful *recently*. One failure had followed another and, in the course of a few months' time, she had come to the only logical conclusion available to her: that she was doomed to fail.

Born Loser?

One of the great things human beings are able to do is to rewrite their own histories. All of us do it all the time. We take a few liberties with the grades we "remember" earning in high school. In filing out an application for employment, we "remember" that we worked at some job or other for a year when, in fact, it was only nine months. We "remember" that we jilted our first girlfriend and that it was not the other way around. These little distortions in what we recall tend to fit our needs at the moment. And, so long as what we remember doesn't harm anyone, no one really much cares how we rewrite our own pasts.

But, consider for a moment, what happens when we are undergoing losses and setbacks and failures at an unprecedented pace? What if things are happening to us that, even though we try to get control of them, we are unable to? And what happens if these things go on and on and on for a period of weeks and months? Do we not begin to feel that we are helpless or that things are hopeless? I think we can.

Now then, since we are all prone to rewriting our own histories couldn't we, when things are at their worst, begin to wonder if we are not losers? And if we are losers today, haven't we always been? And if we have always been losers, doesn't that mean we were *born* losers?

Right or wrong, logical or illogical, once you have decided that you are a born loser, everything in life becomes much simpler—more miserable and more hopeless, but simpler.

No one expects much from born losers. Born losers don't expect much from themselves. Born losers don't expect anything from anyone else. Born losers don't have to try. Born losers don't have to get up in the morning. Born losers don't need to worry about people loving them or them loving others because, as everyone knows, a born loser loses in the love department, too. A born loser, by definition, does not hope—because to do so would be to dream of a better tomorrow. And we all know that born losers do not deserve better tomorrows because, after all, they were born to lose.

If there is a motto for people suffering from hopelessness it is, Born to Lose. And, during the years I consulted for a prison, I saw this motto tattooed on many an inmate's forearm. "Sure I'm a loser," these fellows would say. "Why do you think I'm doing time?"

But there is a terrible price to pay for thinking of oneself as a born loser—and that price is hopelessness. Not only does one begin to live out the self-fulfilling prophecy that says, "Once a loser, always a loser," one must also do everything within one's power to keep this identity going until, one day, one arrives at that place where there is no point in going on.

I don't know who gives birth to losers, but I have yet to meet the parents of one. True, you find parents who tell their kids, "You're nothing and you never will be," but mostly I believe born losers give themselves that dubious title out of a sense of learned helplessness, a sense that no matter what they do, it will make no difference.

So, if you have begun to feel hopeless, please don't take the next seemingly logical step. Don't fall into the trap that says, "Things are hopeless, things have always been hopeless, and, therefore, they will always be hopeless." To do so will require you to take the next step and begin to rewrite your own history so that it makes sense. If you believe the logic that "as things are now, they have always been and will always be," then there must be something wrong with you. And that something is that "*You* must be hopeless."

To qualify as a hopeless case, you will need some kind of new label for yourself, some kind of loser title. Zero man, failure, dud, schlemiel, there are many to choose from. I hope you haven't done this yet. But if you have, maybe it is time to reconsider. Maybe it is time to rethink how you came to feel hopeless and to do something to change this state of mind.

Problems, Problems, Problems

You and I know both know we all have problems. Little ones, daily ones, and those that come in jumbo sizes. Everyone, but everyone, has problems—the rich and healthy, the poor and sick, everyone. It is not possible to live life and not have problems.

But consider for a moment that to the hopeful a problem is a challenge, a chance to find a solution that will work. But to the hopeless, a problem is just another opportunity for defeat. This is the basic difference between the hopeful and hopeless—one sees the problem as an opportunity to win, the other as an opportunity to lose. And therefore, at least in my view, a problem is what you make it.

In my professional work with clients I have come to recognize the earmarks of hopeless thinking and how hopeless people view the problems in their lives. Here are some examples:

"I know I should get out of my marriage, but I'd probably just marry an alcoholic like Fred again."

"I know my job is killing me, but then most people don't like their work. So why should I go to all the bother?"

"I know I ought to lose weight but, shoot, I know myself. I'd just put it on again."

These people are stuck in a hopeless attitude. They see the problem, but they already know the outcome. They know, without a doubt, that they will fail. And so, they ask, why try?

Good question. If I believed as some of my clients do—that there is no outcome to a problem but failure—then I know my work would be useless and I'd be better off selling used cars. But I don't believe my work is useless. And I don't believe my clients are as hopeless as they believe they are. My job, in working with lots of hopeless people, is to shake them up, challenge the way they have come to think about their problems, and to get them to see things differently.

I don't know if you are in this spot or not, but my guess is that if you have been feeling hopeless about your situation, then you may have developed a similar attitude. And, if you have been considering the suicide decision, then I can be almost certain that, at least in some areas of your life, you have chosen to believe that failure is the only sure outcome you can expect.

So, in the rest of this chapter, I want to challenge you on your thinking. I want to shake you up. And, if I can, I want you to consider that, as a human being who has experienced a lot of setbacks lately, you may have rewritten your own history to fit the facts as they seem to you today.

Have you ever wondered why some rich and famous person killed himself? Have you ever wondered aloud, "Why would she? She seemed to have everything, and everything to live for."

A better question might be, "What was she so hopeless about?" Because in asking this question, you would most likely find the answer to the important question. Yes, she had a problem. Yes, it seemed insoluble to her. And, yes, despite her wealth and health and seeming success, she chose the suicide decision. I think if we could know the truth about this person, we would find a feeling of hopelessness had overwhelmed her and that, at the bottom of her final decision, she saw her "problem" as having only one outcome—failure.

It is, then, this sense of certain failure that prompts people to think about suicide. It is this feeling of impending doom, of unavoidable catastrophe, that puts us in the frame of mind where suicide seems so appealing. We can, literally, convince ourselves that defeat is assured and the only thing left to us is to avoid it by killing ourselves.

But wait a minute. I would like to make an alternate case. I would like to make the case that a problem, any problem, can have more than one outcome. Further, I would like to make the case that it is not the absence of problems in our lives that makes us happy, but feeling that we have the power to solve those problems. Problems, in and of themselves, are nothing special. They are as common as rain. And we get them no matter the season. It is not our problems that bring us down; it is, rather, how we think of them and what we do about them that makes the difference.

The Case for Personal Power

Do you remember when you first learned to ride a bike? Remember what a problem it was to get that crazy mechanical device to go on two wheels when, clearly, it needed four? You had to defy nothing less than the law of gravity to stay up there. But what, if you kept trying, finally happened?

Sure, you fell down. Sure, you skinned an elbow or knee. And, yes, you were on the ground more than you were in the air on your first few tries. But then, gradually, you found your balance. You found that you had to keep pumping and going forward if you were to keep from falling down. And then, as if by magic, you made the goofy thing go for a few feet in a semistraight line. Then a hundred feet. Then around the block or down the lane. And soon, within a matter of a few hours, you were feeling like the Master of the Universe, zooming down the road like you owned it.

This feeling, this sense of being the Master of the Universe, is what we all search for in everything we do. It is nothing less than the most wonderful feeling we can know. It is power. It is personal power. It is control. It is taking hold of the problem with both hands and forcing it to scream, "Uncle!" It is, to my way of thinking, the first, best, and only cure for that sense of helplessness and the state of hopelessness.

But learning to ride a bicycle is easy compared to my problems, you say. Anyone can learn to ride a bike, you argue.

Maybe so. But if you could remember back to the first instant you tried to balance yourself on two wheels, I think you would find that that feeling and those you are having now about some other kind of "insurmountable" problem, are exactly the same feelings. The sense of impending disaster, the gut-level knowledge that "it can't be done," and the negative self-talk that says, "I can't do this"—all should be familiar feelings. They accompany most every difficult thing we try for the first time. Such feelings, I would argue, go with the territory of being a member of the human race.

But should such feelings stop us? Because we fall down, should we never try to walk, or to ride a bike, or fall in love? Because a problem is set before us, should we find a way around it or seek to avoid it because we might get hurt? Should we say, "It can't be solved, so why try?"

If you had let those feelings and fears of failure defeat you the first time you got up on two wheels, would you have ever learned to ride a bike? No, of course not.

If you had let your feelings make the decision to go out on a first date, would you have ever gone? Probably not.

If your teacher hadn't encouraged you or insisted that you get up in front of your grade-school class and give your first talk, would you have ever done it? Not likely.

And so it goes with almost anything frightening we ever had to do for the first time. We had to, you and I, do the thing we feared *in spite* of how we felt. We had to act! We had to put our feelings to one side and do the thing! Consequences be damned.

And the next time we did it, we felt a little better. And the next time, a little better still. And by the tenth time we did it, we felt, "Hey, this is easy. What was I so worried about?"

And so the last part of my case is that none of us can afford to have our fears govern our lives. If we let our fears tell us we cannot solve a problem, then is it not an easy thing to say to ourselves, "Why try?" And if we answer our why-try question by not trying, then are we not saying that our case is hopeless?

Out of Hopelessness

Now comes the hard part: How to get out of hopelessness.

My mother was and is a terrific therapist. She has a theory about how to live life that, most likely, grew out of her childhood on an Iowa farm. It went like this: No matter what else you have to do in a day, always accomplish something before breakfast. That way, no matter how badly things go, you can always look back and see that you did something worthwhile and that the day was not a total loss.

And of all things I have read about the treatment of depression and hopelessness, this advice comes as close to the beginnings of a cure as anything the learned professionals have had to say on the subject. Mother's "before breakfast" formula has two important ingredients.

One, you set a small goal and achieve it. It may be washing the car or sewing on a missing button or writing a letter to friend or reading a chapter in a book — almost anything that needs doing for your sake or for the sake of someone else. Whatever it is, it need not be difficult or monumental. It only needs doing. And you get it done! Finished! Complete!

Then, in the second part, at the end of the day (or whenever you feel the dragons are about to devour you), you look back on that small but accomplished goal and say to yourself, "At least I did that today! And on an empty stomach!"

This little antidote for hopelessness is not so little. Because doing something small, achievable, and getting it done (and patting ourselves on the back a bit), gives us something invaluable. And that something is a sense of control and accomplishment. I cannot overemphasize how important these feelings are to each of us, and especially to you if you are feeling a sense of hopelessness. Getting something done, even if it is a small thing, returns power to our lives.

It is very difficult some days to feel that anything any of us do will make any difference at all in the big scheme of things. If you read the newspapers and what is happening or about to happen with pollution, nuclear accidents, wars, famine, the debt crisis, and the fact that what you thought was safe to eat yesterday will cause you to develop cancer tomorrow, it is very easy to fall into a sense of helplessness and, if things begin to go wrong in your personal life, a sense of hopelessness.

But I am not concerned here with whether or not the entire human race is on a collision with itself or that, if we don't change our ways soon, the planet won't be a fit place on which to live. These are things which, even though I try to make some small difference in these conditions each day, I know that I have, in the end, very little control over where mankind is headed or how he is likely to end up. Rather, it is what you and I *do* have control over that concerns me. What we eat, what work we do, how we care for ourselves and others, what we can do to make our lives more interesting and rewarding and challenging and how, however we choose to, we approach our true potential as human beings—these are things that interest me. In a word, the world needs more winners, not losers—born or otherwise.

So, if you would decide to do something about your sense of hopelessness, how might you proceed? Assuming you would not seek out a therapist to help you and that you are not so depressed that the idea of even trying something seems impossible, then I think you might proceed as follows:

(1) Set one small goal for tomorrow. Anything will do. Clean the bathroom. Straighten up a closet or drawer that needs it. Write a letter to someone. Wash, wax, and vacuum the car. Have your hair done. Polish the silver. Call a friend who'd like to hear from you. In a word, set up a surefire goal that you know you can absolutely get done. It can be something you've done a hundred times before.

(2) Then, tomorrow, do it! Don't hesitate. Don't stall. Don't talk yourself out of doing it. Just do it. And use the K.I.S.S. method—which stands for, KEEP IT SIMPLE, STUPID. You don't need to end the cold war or stop hunger in the world or find a new job or a different lover, you just need to wash the car.

(3) Then, when you've done what you set out to do, reward yourself. Not tomorrow. Not next week. I mean right now! You may be out of practice with rewarding yourself, but that is exactly what you need to do. It's nice to have others reward us for our good deeds, but if you haven't noticed lately, a lot of our friends

and family seem to be missing their cues. So, in the short run, you'll need to do this little job for yourself. It doesn't hurt a bit. It may feel a little strange at first, but it doesn't hurt.

(4) Now, for the next day, and the next day, and the day after that, I want you to set more little goals. And more. And then a few more. And, maybe sooner than we know, we'll have the whole house clean, the newspapers tossed out, the car waxed, the drawers all neat and tidy, that novel read, and that call to Aunt Margret made.

(5) At the end of each day and no matter how poorly things have gone or how miserable you seem to feel, force yourself to remember that you accomplished at least one thing that you set out to accomplish for the day. Say to yourself that no matter what else didn't go right, at least I got X done. It will be true. And it should feel good.

If you're getting my drift here, I think you'll see what I'm up to. What I want to happen for you is nothing less than a cure for helplessness and an antidote against hopelessness. Because (and you can call this bootstrap therapy if you wish), I know that if you will start to take these small and seemingly unimportant steps to get control of that part of your life that you *can* control, you will begin to feel that you do, in fact, have some power over your life. And when you accomplish these little tasks, you really do. And no one, but no one, can take that feeling away from you.

More importantly, you will begin to feel that sense of personal mastery returning. And personal mastery, that feeling of being in charge of your own destiny is, from my point of view, as essential to your health—mental and otherwise—as food, water, and air and love.

Then something else will begin to happen. Once you begin to take charge of the little problems in your life, the bigger problems will begin to shrink. Not because they've gotten smaller on their own, but because you are not the same helpless, hopeless person you were a few days or weeks ago. And, if you keep knocking down the little problems, I think you will find the big ones will begin to fall as well.

The reason this will happen is not complicated. And how it happens is not some new and unknown psychological phenomenon. People have been writing and talking about this same process for years. But writing and talking about building self-confidence and self-esteem (or even understanding how one gets hold of one's life), doesn't mean a thing if the persons needing to do this for themselves don't act.

So here is the challenge.

Before you dismiss my suggestions here, I will guess that while you have been reading this you have been saying such things as, "Ah, he makes it sound so easy. It isn't." Or, "If he only knew me, he wouldn't say such dumb things." Or, "This is fine advice for someone else, but not me."

Because, you see, I know you. I know how hopeless people have trained themselves to think. I know that what they have experienced lately has led them to certain negative thoughts—a mode of thinking that is nothing short of deadly. And I know that, within just a few minutes from now, you will try to convince yourself that nothing I've suggested here is worth trying because, after all, I can't possibly know how truly hopeless you are.

That is exactly what I expect you to do. And that's okay. Go ahead and give it your best shot.

But when you've finished trying to convince yourself you can't possibly set one small goal and accomplish it, please consider one more thing: You did just read this entire chapter! You did, in spite of yourself, finish this one small task. Is that not a goal accomplished? Is that not a thing done you set out to do? And, now that you have done it, have you not begun to take some control over your life and exercise some personal power?

Your answer has to be yes.

I don't mean to be clever or to trick you or in any way suggest that by finishing the reading of this chapter you are on your way out of the hopelessness hole. But I will say that by doing this much—however little it may seem—it is still a task that is now done, and that it is a positive thing. And if you will agree with me that it is a positive thing, then I hope you will agree with me that there must be some kernel of hope left somewhere deep inside you. Otherwise, why would you continue reading?

Maybe it would help you to know that many of the most utterly hopeless people I have ever known have managed to keep their therapy appointments with me. And that this single act— despite what their eyes and words said—was proof to me that they continued to hope for some better tomorrow.

And so I hope it is with you and your reading of this book. I know if you will but give yourself the benefit of the doubt and do something positive—be it small, be it insignificant, be it an old familiar routine—the important thing is that you *do* it. Because when you do, when you begin to act on your own behalf, you will begin to feel stronger, think stronger, act stronger, and you will have begun to take the first steps up and out of the hole of hopelessness.

12 _____ …

Drugs, Booze, and Fatal Mistakes

I f you don't now, never have, and never intend to use drugs or alcohol, you might want to skip this chapter. But if you do use drugs or alcohol or prescribed medications (especially sleeping pills, antidepressants or minor tranquilizers), then stay with me.

The reason this chapter is important to you is that if you use any of the above chemicals (especially if you use drugs *and* drink alcohol together) and you are thinking about suicide, then you are walking on a very narrow ledge with your shoelaces untied.

But first I want to ask you to do something: Don't read this chapter if you're high or loaded or stoned right now. I have a rule in my office and it goes like this: I only work with people who bring their whole brain to the appointment. It is difficult enough to come to understand ourselves and to learn new ways of getting on in this world without complicating the job by being high on chemicals. You'd be paying for all of my attention, and I want all of yours.

So, if you're under the influence right now, do yourself a favor and put this book down for now. Then pick it up later when your head is clear. (If you are taking a prescribed medication, okay. I will talk about prescribed medications in a bit later on.)

Good. Now we have two complete brains in the same place. You already know that drugs and alcohol are both powerful and wonderful. Otherwise you probably wouldn't be using them. They can do for our moods what nothing else can. We can eat them, smoke them, drink them, sniff them up our nose, or shoot them in our veins, and the effect is nothing short of miraculous. And we can get this effect within seconds or minutes. With a sufficient dose of what we like, we can feel like gods. We can soar, we can laugh, we can send those blues on the run, we can be with people and feel like nothing can ever hurt us again. With a sufficient dose of what we like, we can feel so good we ask ourselves, "Why should I ever feel bad?"

Now I can guess what you're thinking. You're thinking, well, here it comes, the old drugs-are-bad, drugs-are-dangerous, booze-kills, etc., lecture. You're thinking I'm going to jump up on a soapbox and start preaching against the evils of substance abuse and how, if you would just wake up to the realities of these dangerous substances, you would stop using them this instant.

Well, I'm going to disappoint you. I won't even pretend that I can talk you out of using drugs and alcohol in a book like this. If I thought I could, I would. But I hope I know better than that. I've been working in the substance-abuse field for over twenty years now and if there was a quick cure for people who have found relief or escape though chemicals, I would have invented it a long time ago and registered the patent. Many many years ago I realized that compared to drugs, alcohol, and sex, what a therapist has to offer is pretty thin soup.

This is not to say that treatment for substance abuse doesn't work. It does. But at this moment in your life, I am more concerned about what might happen to you while two dangerous things are going on inside your body; the mixing of suicidal thoughts with alcohol and/or drugs.

So what I do want to talk to you about is drugs, booze, and fatal mistakes. Having assumed you are thinking about suicide and, further, having assumed you drink alcohol or use some kind of drug, I am going to guess that you don't do one without the other. Rather, I'm going to guess that when you are under the influence of the drug of your choice, you may think *more* about ending our life, not less. Or, after coming off a high, you may feel the idea of suicide, compared to the hangover or the downer that follows, has even more appeal.

I'm making these guesses based on what clients have told me.

"When I start to get drunk," Charles said, "I feel real good at first. I feel ten feet tall. I feel like all the problems in my life are small and far away. But then, as the night wears on and the booze wears off, I start to crash. And then I start thinking suicide again."

George was sitting on a bed in hospital and I was talking to him about his suicide attempt. He had gotten drunk, gotten happy, gotten sad, and then gotten mad—mostly at himself for having gotten drunk again.

"What went through your mind before you got the knife?" I asked him.

"I thought . . . let's see. . . . I guess I thought, what the hell, things are never going to be better. I can't even stay sober."

"Do you remember your last words to yourself?" I asked.

George thought a moment. "I think they were, 'What the hell,'" he said.

What the hell. What's the use. Nothing ever gets better, so why try. These are examples of the negative thoughts people often have when they are high or coming down. They are often the same thoughts that go through their heads before they make an attempt on their life.

"Were you drunk when you got the knife?"

"Sure was," said George.

"Would you have stuck that blade into your wrist if you had been cold, stone sober?"

George shuddered. "Hell, no! It would hurt too much!"

Having known lots of people like George, I told him that as much as he might like to kill himself, I doubted very much if he could ever do it sober. And he agreed with me. He agreed that he would have to get good and drunk before he ever tried to kill himself. As he said, "I can't see how anyone can kill themselves unless they're drunk. It's just too painful."

The solution to much suicidal thinking and fooling around with pills and knives and guns and plans to kill yourself can, in my opinion, be solved by simply getting straight and staying that way. I know that may sound simpleminded, but over the years I have met dozens of people whose thoughts about suicide *only* occur when they are intoxicated. It is as if thoughts of self-destruction do not enter their heads unless and until they are under the influence of some drug or other. (By the way, because alcohol and drugs are both drugs, I use the words alcohol and drugs interchangeably.)

Because of what people like George have told me, I know how people can think when they are high. If they are in a good mood when they start to drug, often that good mood gets better. If they are in a bad mood when they start to drink, their mood often gets worse. And if you use enough drugs or alcohol, it's sometimes hard to predict what kind of mood you may end up in—including a suicidal one.

At least two other things happen to us when we get stoned. One, we begin to lose control over our thoughts and actions and, two, things do not frighten us the way they did only a short time before. Alcohol is a solvent and one of the things it can dissolve is fear. Even though this chemical courage only lasts as long as the alcohol is in our bloodstream, while it's there it works pretty well. As one shy young man who made a habit of putting down three or four beers before going to a dance told me, "Why do you think I use the stuff?!"

If we could look our fears right in the face cold sober, many of us probably wouldn't need booze and drugs at all. But fear is fear and, since chemicals do work, you may have developed a dangerous habit of drinking or drugging to deal with what is frightening or painful in your life. And when we've been thinking about our own death (the most frightening proposition of all), it isn't like a hit of some drug or another drink is not going to help. Because it will. That's the one sure thing about drugs and alcohol — they *always* work.

But this is where the risk comes in. If you use a drug or alcohol to change your mood and your changed mood permits you to think more about suicide, then it follows that, while under the influence, you are more likely to do something you would otherwise fear doing — namely, trying to kill yourself.

The research on this, by the way, is quite clear. People who drink and use drugs are at a higher risk of suicide than those who don't. Whether drug and alcohol use leads to suicide or simply permits suicidal people to carry out their plans doesn't really matter to me right now. I'll let the scientists sort that out. What matters to me is that you and I both understand that if you put yourself under the influence and start thinking about suicide, you've greatly increased the odds against your own survival.

Here is another way to think about it.

Cold sober, would you help someone high on drugs to take a fatal dose of heroin? Could you, in your right mind, hand an obviously depressed and drunken woman a razor blade with which to kill herself? Would you, with a clear head, let an angry and brokenhearted friend who was stoned on booze, get into her car and drive home? Of course you wouldn't. You would say, "Hey, sober up! Don't do something crazy! Don't do something you'll regret."

In a word and assuming you too were not stoned, I'm guessing you would do everything within your power to stop an intoxicated friend or stranger who was talking suicide from doing it. Why? Because you know that when they've sobered up or come down, they might not want to kill themselves.

You don't have to be a doctor to know that people under the influence are not packing a full load of bricks. Not only are they two bricks shy of a full load, they don't even know where they left the wagon. And if you don't even know where you left the wagon, how can you decide something as important as whether to live or die?

So, if you wouldn't let some stranger who is high kill himself, why would you fool around with suicide under the same circumstances? Why wouldn't you give yourself the same chance to rethink things with a clear head?

Fatal Mistakes

The other thing I want to talk to you about in this chapter is fatal mistakes. Even sober and straight, we all make mistakes, including fatal ones. We can be distracted and make a left turn in front of a milk truck and that's the last mistake we will ever make. We can dive into a swimming pool on the wrong and shallow end, hit our head on the concrete, and that's that. We can climb up a tree to rescue a stranded kitty, fall out and end up in the next life — probably not liking cats very much.

But these are fatal mistakes over which, because we're sober, we have some control. We might even have been thinking about suicide when we did these things, but it isn't like we set out to die by making some dumb mistake. Not at all.

But now let's add booze or drugs and thoughts of suicide to the dangers of everyday living. Let's go up that tree after the kitty loaded on something. Let's crawl out on that skinny little limb bombed. Have we increased our odds of ending up in a fatal mistake?

Or what about drinking too much and getting behind the wheel of a car? It should come as no surprise that when you have been thinking about killing yourself, drinking, or doing drugs, and get into a two-ton car that can do a hundred miles an hour, you're setting up a situation that is loaded for a fatal mistake. (And you're not doing any of us on the road with you any great favors either.)

Then there are the fatal mistakes that arise out of simply mixing drugs and alcohol. Alcohol in combination with other drugs can be nothing short of deadly. Without going into a complicated explanation of cross-tolerance and drug-potentiation effects, what you need to know is that when you add drugs and alcohol together in your body, a new kind of math takes place. This version of new math can kill you, even though that may not be what you intended to do.

The new math works like this: One ounce of alcohol added to one dose of a drug does not equal two ounces of effect. Far from it. One drug plus one drink might equal four or five or even six ounces of effect. In other words, alcohol can make a drug more powerful and vice versa. This goes for prescribed medications as well, and especially sleeping pills.

One evening in 1974, a twenty-year-old girl drank several gin and tonics and took some pills. The new math took place in her body and she lapsed into a coma, a coma that lasted more than a decade. Her name was Karen Ann Quinlan.

This combination of drugs and alcohol accounts for hundreds of deaths each year, and it is not always clear that the person who died from the new math truly wanted to. Among names you would recognize are Judy Garland, Marilyn Monroe, and Elvis Presley. And for each of these famous names, there are thousands more who only earned a paragraph in the obituary column of their local newspaper.

One of the things that happens when you mix drugs and alcohol or simply start taking sedatives or tranquilizers is that, once the drug begins to take effect, you may begin to lose count of how many pills you have taken. Since short-term memory is affected while under the influence, you may simply lose track of how much of something you have ingested. I don't know about you, but when a doctor prescribes a medicine for me that is supposed to be taken three times a day, I have trouble remembering if and when I took it. And if I have two or more medications to take, I have to write down, count out, or otherwise go to some extra effort just to follow these simple directions. If I were drinking alcohol while taking these pills, I could end up a whole lot sicker than I was when I started.

But the point I most want to make is that if you have been thinking about the suicide decision, you at least ought to do it with a clear head. It is just too easy to slip down into the dumps, start a drinking or drugging episode, let your mind wander off into the seemingly simple solution of suicide, and, because you cannot weigh things out because you've put your brain on the shelf and your fears on the run, you can end up "accidentally" overdosing and dying—maybe quite by mistake.

I know what you're up against with drugs and alcohol. I know what a wonderful tonic these are against bad feelings. I know they work faster than other solutions and that, in them, you can dissolve most anything—anger, depression, hurt, a broken heart, just about anything that is painful. And I know that once you are addicted, the job of getting off the stuff is not something you just up and do one morning before breakfast.

But I also know you can get drug free. It takes some time, it takes some help, and it takes some strength and courage. But you *can* do it.

In the meantime though, since you've been thinking about killing yourself, I want you to know that when you mix drugs or booze with depression and hopelessness and anger and disappointment and whatever else is troubling you, that you are engaging in the most dangerous gamble imaginable. While you may not be entirely sure you want to die, if you put this mixture into your body it is as if, like a coin, you are tossing your life into the air. It may come down heads, you win . . . or it may come down tails, you lose.

I ask you: Is this the kind of high-stakes gamble you want to take?

For my part, and if you were in my office with me, I would now tell you another of my rules: I don't work with suicidal people in therapy while they're using drugs or alcohol. The risk to you is just too great and it is not the sort of gamble I'm willing to take or be a party to. So, if you couldn't stop using drugs or alcohol on your own or with the help of Alcoholics Anonymous or Narcotics Anonymous or some other self-help group (and I mean *right* now), then I would refer you to an inpatient program to help you stop.

This may sound hard-nosed, but if I have learned anything as a psychologist, it is that you and I need both our brains in full working order if we are to work together effectively. More importantly, because I have come to value you as a human being, I wouldn't want you to die by some mistake or miscalculation. Life, yours or mine, is just too dear to lose in the toss of a coin.

13 _____ ...

They Won't Love You
When You're Gone, Either

If you are not living with your parents now, maybe you don't need to read this chapter. Those I want to talk to mostly are young people still living at home. And the reason I want to talk to them is that, in many ways, they are more trapped, more locked in, and maybe feeling more hopeless than those of us who are out in the world on our own.

At the risk of having parents who might read this chapter get angry with me, I'm going to say what I have to say and let the consequences be damned. My obligation in writing this book is to the person who is thinking about taking his or her own life, not to anyone else. So here goes.

As I have said before, I can't know what you're up against. I don't know what kind of parents you have. But I do know a few things about families. And I know a few things about the kind of families in which people begin to think about suicide.

To begin with, our families are supposed to be the place where we can go and feel secure and loved and respected. When the world is against us or we are failing or feeling pushed or threatened, it is to our families we are supposed to turn for support and understanding. Families are supposed to be our port in a storm, our place to go when we have nowhere else to turn. Well, as a lot of us know, this ain't necessarily so!

A boy I knew attempted to hang himself. The rope he tried to use broke and he was unsuccessful. On hearing of this, his father said, "Hell, he can't even do that right!"

A mother brought her daughter to the emergency room after the girl had taken several dozen aspirin tablets in an effort to die.

"She didn't mean it," the mother told the doctor. "It was an accident. She just didn't know what she was doing. She certainly didn't mean to harm herself. Don't worry, after I take her home I'll see to it she doesn't try something like that again. Lord knows we didn't teach her to act like that! I'll ground her for a month!"

Are these loving parents? Probably. Do they know what to do with their suicidal child? Probably not.

As upset as these parents were, each of them did something parents often do when they've had the wits scared out of them — they blamed the victim. It happens all the time. And if you think that by trying suicide you are suddenly going to have loving parents, you might be wrong. You might get their attention and your parents may decide that something is wrong, but there is a good chance that what they will do is decide that something is wrong with you — not them.

Parents Are Not Perfect

For what it's worth, I believe that some adults simply do not know how to be good and loving parents. Maybe their own parents were not loving people and they never had a chance to learn how to be good parents themselves. They certainly don't have colleges where people who want to be parents can go and get training in how to be good parents. Most parents try to be good at their jobs but, let's face it, they don't all get A's in how they raise their children.

So let's talk a little about parents.

First, even though our parents start out to be the most important people in our lives, they don't stay that way. Sooner or later, we come to need them less and less. As we grow up, we find our friends more and more important until, one day, we fall in love with someone and go off and start families of our own. Our families are the starting line in life, not the finish line. And sometimes it helps to remember that while they are our parents, it isn't like we got to pick them.

Immature Parents

I have met lots of moms and dads who were, except for their age, not much older than their children. Emotionally, they were still teenagers. They acted immature and self-centered and generally put their own needs before those of their children. And when their children needed love and understanding, they just couldn't give it, or didn't know how.

So at least one thing you might think about is whether or not your parents even know how to give you what you need. Just because you need them to love and understand you doesn't mean they can or even know how to.

Sometimes our parents were no more than children when they had us. They had dreams and plans and hopes to do something with their lives and, for lots of reasons, maybe they never got to do these things. And so they are frustrated. You and your brothers and sisters started coming along and, before they knew it, they had a family and bills and obligations, and their dreams, however badly they wanted to see them come true, began to disappear.

As sad as it is, some parents begin to blame their children for their own unhappiness. They say, "If I hadn't had you, I could have been . . . " and you can fill in the blanks. Just between me and you, this is a heavy load. And an unfair one. To my way of thinking, each of us is responsible, in large part, for our own happiness. If we don't live our dreams and push for the things we want and take control of our own futures, then we don't have anyone to blame but ourselves. And it is just not right or fair to blame our children for our own shortcomings. But that doesn't mean parents don't do it.

What I want you to understand is that while your parents may blame you for their unhappiness, you don't have to buy it. You don't, as I've seen many kids do, have to accept their blaming you for making their lives miserable.

Because if you do accept this blame, what can you do? Run away? Stop eating food and wearing clothes? Get out of the picture? If you are the one who is holding them back from their dreams and making them unhappy, then maybe the thing to do is to relieve them of this burden (you) and kill yourself.

Maybe you have thought, "If I just killed myself, my mother could be happy. She could go back to school and do all the things she says she wants to do. I'm just in the way."

But let me suggest something to you. What if I told you that your mother's happiness is her job, not yours? What if I told you that even if you killed yourself, she would probably not be happy and, in fact, she would be more unhappy. Because now, in addition to whatever other failures she has had, your killing yourself makes her a complete failure as a mother.

Even though parents may say things that make you feel like you are a burden to them, it doesn't necessarily follow that if you exit the scene, they are suddenly going to grow up and take responsibility for their own happiness. And if I had to bet on what they would do after your suicide, it would be that they would simply find someone else to blame for why they don't live up to their dreams.

Killing yourself to get out of the way is no solution to your parents' unhappiness. Their unhappiness is *their* problem, not yours.

Angry Parents

The lack of love and understanding from immature parents is one kind of pain a child sometimes has to live with, but there is something worse. Sometimes your parents are angry and hostile and openly fight with each other. Sometimes they seem to be at war with one another and they may even hit each other. There is name-calling and swearing. There may even be threats to kill each other. Or one parent may threaten suicide to get back at the other. A kid caught in a family where violence is present or violence is threatened is in a very tough spot and it isn't hard to understand how such a child may begin to think about getting out of the war zone by the suicide escape route.

In families like this, it is very difficult to grow up. Sometimes these kinds of parents don't want you to grow up. Sometimes they need you there, right in the middle, to help them buffer the fights. Sometimes your father may come to you and ask that you side with him against your mother. Or the other way around. These are terrible choices and no one should be forced into making them, but that doesn't change things. And if you are caught in a family like this and thinking about suicide, you need to know that you are not alone. All kinds of kids caught in families like this think about suicide as a way out.

One of the things that happens to kids caught in angry families like this is that the parents may say, "If it wasn't for the kids, I'd leave!" Or, "If it wasn't for these damned kids, I would have left you years ago!"

When you hear this, what do you think? What you think is that you're standing in the way of what they say they want. They say they want their freedom and you are their ball and chain. You start feeling like a fifth wheel or a third thumb. You start wondering what you can do to solve *their* problems.

For good reason, lots of kids begin to assume that they are the source of their parents' problems with each other and that, if they simply got out of the picture, their parents would be able to be happy and be back in love with each other. And, what's worse, the parents let them think this way.

Sharon was a seventeen-year-old girl whose parents sent her to see me because she was having trouble at school. She was feeling panicky and couldn't concentrate. Always a good student, she was failing three classes. She was having trouble getting to sleep.

The last child of three, she was the only one still at home. Because her problems seemed to be getting worse and worse, she had begun to think that maybe she should kill herself.

"Why do you think you should kill yourself?" I asked her.

"Because it would solve everything."

"What things?"

"Everything."

"Like what?"

"I could get out," said Sharon. "I could get out for good."

"Get out of what?"

"School. Home."

I knew that Sharon had been a good student. She had been active in sports and was on the debating team. She had always liked school. "Tell me about what's happening at home," I suggested.

Sharon started to cry.

Then she told me the story. Her father had been having an affair with another woman and, about three months earlier, her mother had found out about it. There had been a terrible fight. There was no hitting, but her mother had threatened to kill herself if her father didn't stop seeing the other woman. Sharon had overheard them quarreling one night. She had heard her mother say, "If it wasn't for Sharon, I'd kill myself." And her father had said, "Don't let that stop you!" And her mother said, "Oh, I wouldn't do it right now. I'll wait until she goes away to college."

But in front of Sharon, her parents acted as if nothing was wrong. They went on with their family life and pretended that everything was fine. But of course everything was not fine. Sharon, being a good kid and wanting nothing more than her parent's happiness, did what any kid would do: she began to think about what she could do to keep her mother alive.

One of the things she decided to do was not go away to college. She reasoned that as long as she stayed home, her mother would not kill herself. In doing this, she was making herself a prisoner. All she had to do was sacrifice her happiness, her future, and her life. But the plan was not working. And because it was not working, she had begun to think of suicide.

I asked Sharon what she had hoped to major in at college.

"Psychology," she said. Then she smiled. "I guess I want to be able to help them."

"You're already helping them," I said, "you're just not getting paid."

I knew I had the wrong patient in my office and told Sharon so. Then I called her parents and asked them to come in. In time, we were able to work everything out and the family stayed together. Sharon went away to college the next year and no one had to commit suicide.

The point of Sharon's story is that, like a lot of other kids caught between their parents, she had come to believe that she alone was responsible for keeping them together and, in Sharon's case, for keeping her mother alive.

Dying for Attention

Margie was eighteen when I first met her. She was pretty and small and had long blonde hair. Even though it was summertime she wore a long-sleeved blouse. She wore long sleeves year-round. Long sleeves helped cover the scars on her wrists, of which she had several.

For most of her young life, Margie had been unhappy. Her mother had divorced her father when she was ten and, as many single parents do, her mother had begun dating other men in hopes of finding someone with whom to share her life. But her mother's search had been unsuccessful and, she too, was unhappy. Margie's mother began to drink and spend weekends away from the apartment with her dates. Margie was left alone and, neglected and ignored, she began to wonder if her mother really loved her. She began to wonder that if she were not in the picture, would her mother find another husband.

"The first time I cut myself was on a Sunday morning," she said. "I must have been about twelve. Mother had been gone since Friday night and I didn't know where she was. When she finally came home, she found me bleeding."

"What happened then?" I asked.

"Oh, she got very upset. She cried and said she loved me and that she would never leave me alone again."

"Did she?"

"Yes. It only lasted a couple of weeks. She bought me some new clothes and took me out for pizza. But then she started going out again and staying away for the weekends."

"What did you hope would happen when you cut yourself?"

"I don't know," said Margie. "I guess I hoped she would stay home and be with me. Or just care about me. But she's so wrapped up in her own life. It's like I don't exist."

"Did you want to die?"

Margie thought a moment. "I guess so. At least I didn't want to live anymore."

Margie had cut her wrists several times, each time a little deeper and a little more seriously. And each time her mother came home to find her bleeding, there were hugs and kisses and promises that things would be better. But these promises didn't last.

Margie and her mother were caught in a suicide game, a game in which one person has to threaten to kill herself in order to get the other person to pay some attention and prove that, indeed, she loves her.

This is a dangerous game in which there are never any winners. Eventually, everyone loses. I don't know why or how a parent could be so wrapped up in her own life as to ignore a child who needs attention and love and time and understanding, but such parents are a fact of life and, if you happen to have one, then you need to know that you are not alone. And, since your parent may not be able to give you the love and time you need, you may have to be the one who has to be tolerant and understanding and, in a way, more mature.

If You Think They Don't Love You

I can't know if your parent or parents, down deep, really love you. Maybe you can't tell either. Chances are, they do. But I do know this: threatening to take your life or making an attempt to kill yourself will not bring you any proof of their love. Yes, attempting to kill yourself will get their attention. Yes, attempting suicide will wake them up to the fact that something is wrong. But attempting to kill yourself will not necessarily lead to any permanent changes. And there is a big risk here.

It is quite possible that if you attempt to kill yourself your parents will love you less, not more. If you try to kill yourself and fail, they may be angry with you. They may be frightened of you. They may not want to leave you alone for fear you will try again. And, of this I am sure, they will resent the way you have tried to make them prisoners.

Prisoners? Yes.

When you attempt to kill yourself to get someone's attention or to get someone to say she loves and cares for you, you have used the most powerful weapon any of us can ever use — and that weapon is your life. If you are willing to die to get what you want, then you stand a very good chance of getting *some* of what you want. You will get attention. You will get people to listen. But they will do so not because they suddenly discovered they love you, but because they are afraid of losing you or of being disgraced if you kill yourself.

So what, really, have you done? Have you not said, "If you won't love me, I will kill myself!"

If you do this, the people you do it to will feel threatened and trapped. They will feel that you have taken them prisoner. They will feel that if they do not do exactly what you want them to do, then you will kill yourself and they will be to blame. It is an emotional prison you have put them in, but a prison all the same.

Once you have put your parents (or anyone else) in such a

prison, one thing is sure to happen. Even though they may not be able to admit it, they are going to start to dislike you. They may even come to hate you for the way you are controlling them by your threats to kill yourself. And no one likes to be controlled.

Not long ago I heard of a boy whose mother was threatening to leave home and divorce his father. The boy told his mother that if she did that, he would kill himself. He said this many times. And, each time he said it, his mother would waver in her decision to leave. Then, after threatening to kill himself one more time if his mother moved out, she became angry and said, "Why don't you stop talking about it and go ahead and do it! It won't change my mind."

The boy killed himself that same night.

The end of this story is not happy either. Right after the funeral, the mother moved out—just as she had planned.

So what I want you to think about is that no matter how badly you may need love and understanding from your parents, threatening to kill yourself won't get them. If anything, your threats may only make things worse. And, secondly, if you have come to believe that your parents' marriage will somehow be saved if you die, you will be making a big and permanent mistake. They may need help, but your death is not it.

The last thing I want to tell you about is that, at least in some families, you may be expected to kill yourself. Your parents may not say, in so many words, "Why don't you just kill yourself," but they may, by their actions, be suggesting that the family would be just as well off if you weren't there.

I know how unlikely this sounds, but I have seen it more than once.

Tom was eleven years old when his Uncle John committed suicide. It was a family tragedy and made a powerful impression on him. Later, when Tom was in high school his father had become angry at him for bringing home poor grades. "You're a loser just like your Uncle John," his father had said, "and you know what he did!"

Hurt and upset, Tom interpreted this to mean that he, too, should commit suicide rather than fail in school. And while he hadn't actually tried to kill himself, not a day had gone by since his father's statement that he hadn't thought about it.

I don't know whether Tom's father knew what impact his comparing Tom to an uncle who killed himself had had on Tom, but the effect on Tom had been devastating. It was as if he had been given a death sentence. Each time Tom's father was angry with him for anything, Tom immediately thought of killing himself.

I don't know if Tom's father really wanted him dead and out of the picture. I doubt it. But then maybe he did. It would not be impossible. Some parents have, in fact, wished their children dead. But the thing to remember is that parents can say and do things that, if they would stop to think about the impact of their words or actions, they might regret. And even if they do not regret them and mean what they say, it is still *their* problem, not yours!

Finally, I want you to know this: Once you are born you have a right to life—as much right as anyone else. The law says so and everyone who upholds the law will do everything within his power to see to it that you keep your rights to life. No one, not even your parents, can take those rights away from you.

So, if by chance you have been born into a family where your parents really don't want you or where they don't know how to love you or where you have come to believe that you have to die to please someone or to make someone happy, then please remember these things:

You are the one who counts most.

You are not so much the child of your parents as you are the product of life itself.

You are the world that is to be.

And, as I said in the beginning, they won't love you when you're gone, either.

14 _____ ...

For Those Who Have Tried

After thinking about who might read this book, I realized that at least some of you may have already made a suicide attempt. Maybe you are sitting in a hospital dayroom with fresh stitches in your wrist. Or maybe you are at home alone. Maybe no one knows that you have just tried to end your life. I can't know your circumstances, but because I have some idea of what you might be going through, I want to talk with you about what you have tried to do and what I think it means to have done it.

From a statistical point of view, many experts believe that once you have attempted suicide, you are now at a higher risk of attempting it again and, maybe one day, of succeeding. If I can, I want to try to reduce that risk to you.

Since I cannot know what has happened in your life that brought you to the decision to end it, I cannot talk about these things except in the most general of terms. So what I want most to do is to talk with you about what you might be going through in these hours and days after you have tried to kill yourself and to help you understand that, once you have tried to commit suicide, it does not mean that you must or will try it again.

Your Reactions

Many people who have unsuccessfully tried to end their lives feel as though they have, as in everything else lately, failed again. Some of them are angry with themselves. They feel confused and guilty. They feel stupid and foolish and as though, even though they tried to do the one thing that would make things better, they ended up making things worse.

More than one person who has recently attempted suicide has said to me, "I've really made a mess of things now, haven't I?"

And, to be candid, sometimes they have. I will talk about some of the possible consequences of an unsuccessful suicide attempt in another chapter, but for now I want to focus on what you might be going through and what you can learn from what has happened.

Most everyone I have talked to has felt, in the hours right after his attempt, frightened by what he did. In the days or hours just before they made the attempt, many of them felt some sense of control over their immediate future, as if they finally had mastered the situation that seemed so impossible. Some of them felt a certain calm or serenity in the final hours before they tried to end their lives.

But after their attempt had failed they suddenly felt that sense of control slip away, as if they were once again thrown back into the chaotic world they had just tried to escape. They found the world had not changed for the better, and sometimes it seemed even worse. Then, as they began to accept the fact that they did not die, they became frightened by the power of their own emotions—emotions that could push them to an act of self-murder.

Some people have reported a sense of relief at having survived a suicide attempt. Many have told me that they were glad they didn't die after all, that they were glad they thought to save themselves at the last minute or that others were there to rescue them from their attempt. Still others have felt just the opposite.

"Why did they bother to save me?" Mary said. "I wanted to

die. Why couldn't they just let me go? Couldn't they see that's what I wanted?"

Mary had taken a lethal overdose and, had it not been for the heroic work of the doctors and nurses, she would have died. She was angry with the hospital staff. She swore at them. They had foiled her plans and forced her to live.

Until I met Mary, I had never known anyone who was so insistent on killing herself. She had made up her mind, made her plans, and carried them out. Only by a stroke of luck (a neighbor dropped by to borrow a *TV Guide*) had she been found unconscious and rushed to the hospital.

In the weeks that followed Mary's suicide attempt, she remained angry—angry at herself, angry at the people who had saved her, angry at the judge who ordered her to see me, angry at me for trying to convince her life was better than death, and angry at the world in general.

But in time Mary came to understand her anger; its source, its meaning, and learned that she could turn her anger into energy for positive change. Mary's anger, in the end, was the thing that saved her.

In many ways Mary had a right to be angry with life, but only with help did she gradually come to understand that she was not to blame for all the things that had gone wrong in her life. In time she began to see that killing herself was only *one* way she could deal with her anger. There were other, more productive ways to use anger and, as we worked together, she found ways to retarget her anger and to express it in healthy, purposeful directions.

Many months after her suicide attempt Mary said, "I guess I was mad at the wrong person. But that doesn't mean I'm not still mad. This is still a pretty lousy world."

These ten years later, I still get a Christmas card from Mary. She's still angry, but at least she no longer blames herself for everything that goes wrong.

For some, one suicide attempt is enough. One brush with the

real possibility of dying is enough to jar the person into a new plane of reality. Many people have recovered from their suicidal crisis and attempt, decided that the reason they thought they wanted to die was not a good enough reason, and then gone on about the business of living with a bold new vision of what life could be. As one young woman told me after attempting to kill herself over the loss of a boyfriend, "To think, I almost killed myself over that bum!"

For others, though, the first suicide attempt becomes a haunting memory, a set of negative thoughts that hound them each time they find themselves hurt or depressed or lonely. They have attempted the ultimate solution once and, having tried it once, they sometimes feel compelled to try it again. This, in my view, is the curse of the self-fulfilling prophecy.

A self-fulfilling prophecy is, simply, a belief that one has a certain destiny and that, no matter what else you may do, you are bound to live out that destiny. If, for example, you believe that you will one day die by your own hand and you never challenge that belief or seek to change it or discard it, then that belief hangs there somewhere in the back of your consciousness, waiting until just the right set of circumstances. And then, when the chips are down and the desperation begins, BOOM! Here comes that old thought: "I must kill myself!"

A philosopher once said, "The thought of suicide is a great consolation; by means of it one gets successfully through many a bad night." This statement, to me at any rate, is an example of how thinking about suicide can be both a relief and potential enemy. It is a relief for all of us to know that we have the power to end our own suffering any time we wish, but such a thought becomes an enemy if we believe such an idea carries the force of our own self-imposed law. It is as if one is saying, "I know that if things get bad enough, I can always kill myself." This is very different from the thought, "I know that if things get bad enough, I *must* kill myself!"

So even though you may have tried suicide once, it does not necessarily follow that you must, sooner or later, take your own life. If life is a play and you are the scriptwriter, then who says you can't change act 3? Who says you can't rewrite the ending to your own play? Simply put, and even though your life has been running like a Greek tragedy recently and your suicide attempt is proof positive of that fact, it doesn't mean it has to end that way. You might, as I frequently do with my clients, ask yourself a question, "Who's writing this play anyway?"

The Reaction of Others

I want to talk briefly about how others may react to your suicide attempt. And I want to do this so that, if you have recently made an attempt, you will know something of what others might be feeling or thinking.

First, there is no single or predictable reaction to a suicide attempt. Some people will show immediate sympathy and understanding. Others will be angry with you, as if you have done something to hurt or embarrass them. Some may be ashamed of you, ashamed that you could have done something so terrible to yourself and against God.

One reaction is almost always predictable: you will have frightened those who know and love you. How they handle their fear of your life-threatening act will vary, but you can bet that because you made an attempt to end your life, they have been put in fear—a fear that is partly out of their concern for you and partly out of concern for themselves.

"He didn't really mean to hurt himself," the father of a teenage boy said. "He was just fooling around."

The boy in question had attempted to hang himself and was found just as he was losing consciousness. But there was no question that he had made a suicide attempt.

The father, out of his need to deny that anything could be wrong with his son or himself or his family, hoped to deny to himself and anyone who would listen that everything was not fine.

Denial is a major psychological defense against fear and anxiety and all of us use it at one time or another. Unexamined and unchanged, the denial by others of your suicide attempt is never helpful to you or them. It is as if someone has said, "You did not really try to kill yourself. Why don't we all agree to forget the whole incident?" This conspiracy of silence, in my experience, does no one any good and, if anything, only increases the likelihood that the reasons you sought to end your life will remain a mystery—except to you.

And, if you go along with those who hope to "forget" the whole thing, you will be left alone with the very same problems you had before and, therefore, the very same thoughts about how to correct them. So if there is a time for you to break out of this conspiracy of silence, now is the time to do it. If you must, go outside your family or your circle of friends and find someone who can understand what you have tried to do so that, with objective help, you can find a better solution than suicide.

Some of those around you will deal with their fear by becoming angry with you and blaming you for what you have tried to do. They may say something like, "Look what you have done to me!" Or, "How could you be so stupid?!"

Maybe this is the reaction you expected to get. Maybe you were mad at them and your suicide attempt was a way to let them know just how mad you were. Maybe you set out to prove that whoever is mad at you really didn't love you anyway and, now that you have tried to kill yourself, you have proof for your belief. I don't know. But I do know that if that is what you set out to prove and have now proved it, then I hope one test of their love is enough and that you don't, later and again, feel the need to test them again.

The Best Outcome

What I hope has happened (or will happen) for you if you have attempted suicide, is that some change will take place in your life, some positive change. The reasons people attempt suicide are many, but I think all who try have some hope that by dying or threatening to die they can bring about some change in the way things are. They hope to end their suffering, their pain, their loneliness, or to stop the steady flow of losses in their lives. Their attempt to suicide had a reason and, at least in their minds, a good one.

So if you have attempted to end your own life I hope, for your sake, that good things will now begin to happen. I hope that now that you have survived the crisis, you will see this is a time to look to new beginnings, new possibilities, new opportunities, and new relationships. An attempt on your own life need not, automatically or in that awful power of the self-fulfilling prophecy, lead to another attempt. Rather, I hope that your suicide attempt can be an opportunity for a new start, a rebirth if you will.

Terry, a good friend of mine who attempted suicide when he was a young man, said to me when he learned I was writing this book, "Paul, I didn't start to live until after I'd tried to die."

I won't pretend that everyone who has tried to kill himself can just jump up running and change his whole life in the twinkling of an eye. Few can do this. But with help and time and a realization that life can be more than it has been, I have no doubt that you can find at least some of that which you seek. Be it love, or success, or happiness, I am certain of at least one truth: these things are only available to the living.

15 _____ ...

What If You Don't Succeed?

I had a long debate with myself about whether or not to write this chapter. On the one hand, what I have to say to you here is both unpleasant and, some might argue, unnecessary. On the other hand, I promised you an honest book. Since most people who attempt suicide do not succeed, I feel I would be cheating you if I didn't share what I know about what can happen if you try to kill yourself and fail to get the job done. So, I will keep my promise.

The first time I realized that suicide was something less than a sure thing and not a slick and easy way to solve one's problems, I was interviewing a man who had just been admitted to a psychiatric ward. We'll call him Charles.

Charles had been depressed for many months. A middle-aged man, he had been out of work for most of a year and his unemployment checks had stopped. He had a family to feed and, try as he might, he could find no solution to his crisis. From his point of view there was only one decision left to him: suicide. He had reviewed his life-insurance policy and found that there was no restriction on the payment of his death benefit if he should die by his own hand. Upon his death, his family would receive several thousand dollars, dollars he hoped would keep them going in his absence.

The day he was admitted to the hospital Charles had gotten up early and gone into the bathroom with his hunting knife — a knife with a long sharp blade. He took off his shirt. He placed the point of the blade between two ribs over what he thought was his heart and, with the force of both hands, jammed the blade inward as hard as he could.

But Charles missed his heart. His missed it by a fraction of an inch. "The pain was terrible," he said. "And the blood went everywhere. It ruined the carpet."

I was a young psychologist when I met Charles and, frankly, his story made me wince. It frightened me to imagine a man could be so depressed and desperate as to shove a knife into his chest for a few thousand dollars. Until that moment I, maybe like you, had always thought of suicide as a neat and tidy act where, after the person has died, you would see him lying in a casket like anyone else — all visible signs of trauma to the body carefully concealed from friends and family by the mortician's skill.

But here was a man in a full chest bandage talking calmly about how he wished he'd known better where his heart was so that he could have cut it open and died.

"I should have shot myself," said Charles, "but I needed some cash and had to hock my guns a few months back."

Charles's wife had found him lying on the bathroom floor in a pool of blood and, with the help of her sons, they managed to get him to an emergency room where the surgeons removed the knife, sutured him, and sent him on to the psychiatric floor. He was alive now, but not out of danger, and it wasn't until several months later that, with the help of the staff and a vocational rehabilitation plan that would train him in a new profession, that Charles was able to return to his home and family.

Humans Are Hard to Kill

Most people contemplating suicide do not realize how difficult it is to kill a human being. We're actually made of pretty tough stuff and despite what you may see on television or in the movies about how easily people can be killed, it doesn't happen that way in real life. Maybe, because of our exposure to these fictional versions of dying and our willingness to believe death is simple, we don't want to understand that dying can be both difficult and painful. Charles found this out the hard way, and so have thousands of others who have tried to kill themselves.

True, there are some methods of self-murder that are more successful than others. But even the most lethal methods can fail. Consider what happened to the following people—all of whose identities have been changed to protect the real person:

Tom, a teenage boy, put a .22 pistol to his head and pulled the trigger. The bullet entered his temple, ripped through his brain, ricocheted around the inside of his skull, and lodged in his jaw. He did not die. Now severely brain-damaged, he lives on—unable to work or go to school.

Mary jumped from a high bridge into a river. Many people have died making this same jump. Mary did not. Rather, she entered the water at a bad angle and broke her back. She was rescued before she could drown. Mary lives in a wheelchair.

George shot himself with a large-caliber pistol in the stomach. He destroyed a kidney. Fortunately, he had two.

Bryan, arrested on a drug charge and fearful of his parents' reaction, attempted to hang himself in jail. He succeeded only in strangulating himself and losing consciousness. The loss of oxygen to his brain caused permanent brain damage.

Janice cut her wrists—sideways. One of the cuts ran deep enough to sever a tendon. Janice used to play the piano. She still plays, but not so well.

I could go on, but I think I've made my point.

If you think about suicide attempts the way we counselors do, you would know that there are serious, first-degree attempts, second-degree attempts, and third-degree attempts. First-degree suicide attempts are planned, deliberate, premeditated acts involving the most lethal means. Second-degree attempts are more impulsive, unplanned, and not as well thought out. Third-degree attempts are those in which the person deliberately puts himself in a dangerous situation in which he may die, but his intent is not so clear. But all attempts, even very serious, first-degree ones, do not guarantee results.

Maybe these fine distinctions don't matter to you. Or maybe you haven't thought through all the possibilites. But if you are thinking about killing yourself, please be aware of at least one other potential outcome: *You may not die!*

The general rule is that the more lethal the method you try, the more damage your body will sustain and the greater the likelihood that you will end up disfigured or disabled if your attempt fails. As cold and hard as that sounds, it is nonetheless true.

Overdoses of pills can lead to respiratory failure and may cause a coma from which you may never recover.

A high-speed crash in a car may leave you a cripple for life.

Slashing your wrists will not only leave scars, but you may permanently damage the tendons and muscles that control your hands.

As Tom and others have learned, even a pistol shot to the head does not guarantee death.

As heartless as it may sound, I have heard doctors and nurses say of someone they have just managed to save from death and who they know will now be permanently disfigured or handicapped, "Maybe they would have been better off dead." And please remember that because of modern lifesaving methods and technology, the doctors are saving more and more people who, only a few years ago, would have died of their self-inflicted injuries.

As some suicide attempters have learned, a failed attempt can be a double curse. Not only have they failed to do what they set out to do but now, in some cases, they no longer have the means or freedom or physical ability to finish the job. They may find themselves confined to a bed in a nursing home, unable to care for themselves and prisoners of their own making. And, once the treatment staff know that you have made a suicide attempt, they will take every possible precaution to see to it that you do not try again.

You will not be permitted to have anything sharp in your possession—no knives to cut your meat, no razor to shave with. They may not let you have a belt to hold up your pants. You will not be permitted into a bathroom alone. You will be put on what is called a "suicide watch" and you will have very little, if any, privacy. In a word, no one will trust you for fear you will try to kill yourself again.

Even if the consequences of a failed suicide attempt are not so disastrous as a lasting disability or confinement to a nursing home or mental hospital, there are other unpleasant consequences.

Ann was a fifteen-year-old girl when she first cut her wrists. She helped make me aware of another problem I hadn't, at the time I met her, thought of.

"I have to wear long-sleeved blouses all the time," she said. "Even in the summer. When those big, clunky bracelets were in, I could sometimes get by. They would just cover the scars—provided no one looked too close. I never go swimming or to the beach because you can't hide these scars when you're in a bikini."

Ann told me that when people did notice the scars on her wrists, they would sometimes innocently ask, "What happened to your wrist?" Then, realizing how such scars are usually gotten, they would catch themselves and apologize. "It's very embarrassing," Ann said. "You feel like you have to make up some story—otherwise they'll think the worst."

I know that what I have said here may amount to some kind of scare tactic, that I'm trying to frighten you out of your thoughts about the suicide solution. And, in a way, I suppose I am. But because I have met so many people who have attempted suicide and failed, I thought I ought to share with you what I have seen and heard and learned from others.

I know it is not enough just to warn people who want to kill themselves that, if they try, they may not succeed and some terrible unanticipated consequence may follow. But because I know that once you are in that terrible and lonely place and in the midst of that awful crisis of whether to live or die, you may convince yourself that the solution you seek will be neat and clean and tidy and final. This is part of the logic of suicide: that death will be quick and easy.

But I will quote Murphy's Law, "If a thing can go wrong, it will." And Murphy's Law, I'm afraid, applies just as well to suicide attempts as anything else.

Other Consequences

Beyond the possible damage to your body if you fail to die in your attempt, there are a host of other complications. Most of these have to do with the way people will react to your attempt, how you will feel and think about yourself, and how your life will change as a result of not dying. I have tried to write about some of these consequences elsewhere in this book. But here, for now, I simply wish to remind you that a suicide attempt is like throwing a stone into a quiet pool — the impact of the stone sends ripples far and wide, ripples that affect you and everyone you know. And that effect is often an unknown one, one which neither I nor anyone else can predict.

Finally, I hope that what I have said here does, in fact, put a bit of uncertainty into your thinking about suicide. Perhaps if I can convince you that your best-laid plans can go awry and that you just could end up in much worse shape than you can possibly imagine, then maybe you will think twice about killing yourself.

One thing I know: if you can hold on and get through the troubled times you are going through you will, sooner or later, come to realize that you are stronger than you think. You will, in years to come, look back on this crisis as just that — a crisis like many others you have survived and will survive.

There is, in my opinion, nothing romantic or mysterious or

enviable about dying by suicide. And, failing to die by suicide is not only unromantic, it is a sad and tragic irony. If the newspapers printed all the stories about what happens to people like Tom and Charles and Ann and the thousands of others whose plans to suicide have failed and who have ended up crippled or disfigured or disabled, it just might cause all of us to think, not twice, but three times before we tried to kill ourselves.

As Ann said to me, "Tell them not to try. It's stupid."

16 ...

The People You Leave Behind

You may not like what I have to say in this chapter. And it may make you feel a bit guilty about the thoughts you have given to ending your own life. But that is okay with me. As I said in the beginning, I promised you an honest book. So, even though you may not like what you are about to read, I've decided that there is no point going this far without going all the way. And all the way includes the answers to the "what if" questions. As in, "What if I killed myself?"

Some people might argue that talking about what happens to the people you leave behind if you kill yourself may invoke more guilt in you than you can handle. I don't believe this is true. What I do believe is that if you intend to take your own life, then you ought to know, as much as is possible, what *all* the consequences of such an act are, including the likely consequences to others if you succeed.

Who are the others? They are your parents, your brothers and sisters, cousins, aunts and uncles, friends and loved ones, the people at school, the people at work—literally everyone who knows you. Because no other word describes them as well, the professionals in my field have chosen to call these people victims. Survivors of suicide, they are victims because, to one degree or another, they will suffer because you have suicided. Some of them will need love and understanding to recover from the tragedy of your death. The closer they are to you, the more they will suffer. And none will suffer more than your family.

I have talked to many suicidal people who lie to themselves. They lie to themselves because they need to, because it is the only way they can justify killing themselves, knowing, as maybe all suicidal people do, that when they intend to hurt themselves, they will also hurt others. Here is how one young girl lied to herself.

"I see myself lying in a casket. I am in my blue dress and my hands are folded over my chest. I can see my parents and my friends standing around me. They are crying."

"What are they saying?" I asked.

"They are saying how beautiful I look, how peaceful I seem. My sister is saying, 'I know Renée is happy now.'"

"What else are they saying, Renée?"

"That they will miss me."

"Are they saying they wish you hadn't killed yourself?"

"No."

"Are any of them angry?"

"No."

At this point I interrupted what we call a guided fantasy and brought Renée back to the real world. I brought her back to tell her what her funeral scene might really be like. Yes, her parents and sister and friends would be crying and saying those thoughtful things about how peaceful she looked, that she was still, in death, so young and beautiful and, yes, wasn't it a shame that she had died before her life really began? But underneath all of these carefully worded expressions of love and affection, something else is going on in her victims' hearts and minds.

They are shocked. They cannot believe what has happened. They are numb and in pain. It is as if they are caught up in a nightmare and, when they awake, the nightmare goes on and on. Feeling confused and dazed, they wonder if they will ever get over your death or if things will ever be normal again.

They are sad. Once the shock and the numbness wears off, the survivors of suicide enter a time of great and unremitting sadness. Unprepared as they are, the pain can be almost physical, and despite an occasional good day or light moment, the sadness sweeps over them, again and again.

They are angry. Though they wish not to be, they cannot but feel anger toward you. You have taken something precious from them and there is no getting it back. They are angry with you for cheating them, for rejecting them, for not giving them a chance to help you heal from what was troubling you. If they were in the wrong, then by your death you have taken away any opportunity for them to try to make things right.

They can't apologize now. They can't learn to listen now. By your suicide, you have deprived them of any chance to understand you or to love you. And so they feel a terrible anger toward you — an anger that will fade in time, but will be there, in the back of their minds, for the rest of their lives.

And because of this anger, they will feel guilt. They know it is wrong to be angry with you, but they will feel this anger anyway. And when they do, they will feel guilty for being angry with you.

This is no passing guilt. This is guilt that will haunt them, not for just a week or a month, but for the rest of their lives. They will wonder what they did wrong, but they will also wonder why you chose to hurt them as you did. They may come to hate God as well. And they will feel guilt about this, too.

Their life will never be the same. Once you have killed yourself, it is as if you have taken all the happy photographs of you in your family's album and written the word SUICIDE in black letters across your face. Nothing, but nothing, will ever be the same for them again.

Among the things that can happen to those you leave behind are the following:

They may become suicidal themselves. Out of a need to escape the pain they are feeling, they may wonder if suicide is a good solution for them, too. Some survivors have even thought to kill themselves to join the one who has suicided.

They may feel they are going insane or losing control. Their world has been suddenly and inexplicably turned upside down and shattered and, as was true of Humpty Dumpty, no one and nothing seems able to put Humpty Dumpty together again.

Because of the shame they feel, they may not be able to turn to anyone to talk to through their pain. They may begin to use drugs or alcohol. They may go into a long and life-threatening depression. At the very least they will feel guilt and anger and confusion. They will try to remember the way you were when you were happy and they will try to salvage what memories of your life they can. But there will always be that unbearably sad ending—an ending that they can do nothing to erase.

If you are a father or a mother, you will have left something very much like a curse on your children. The curse reads: "I have killed myself. You may wish to do the same some day. By my act, you have my permission."

If you are a child, you will have stolen something from your parents, something they can never replace. You will have stolen the future they dreamed for you, the satisfaction that might have come to them to see you grow into an adult and succeed where they may have failed. One father said of his only son's suicide, "He has stolen my grandchildren from me. He has put an end to our family name."

If you are a husband, you will have said of your marriage, "*She* failed me!" Or, if you are a wife, your suicide might say, "Look how *he* treated me! I had to kill myself!" Either way, the one you once loved may never be able to forgive you for the way you publicly denounced your relationship. Maybe their distress is what you want. I don't know. But if it is, your own life is a high price to pay for striking back in anger.

If you are a brother or a sister, you will have said that no matter how close you were to each other, you were not close enough. And you will have set for them an example. A friend of mine whose brother attempted to kill himself said to me, "I was so mad at him, I threatened to kill him myself if he ever tried something like that again."

There is one other thing your survivors will experience: sudden loss, sudden pain, and sudden grief. There is a difference between natural and unnatural death. The one we can bear and learn to live with because, as we become aware of death through the natural death of someone we know and love, we come to accept our own deaths and hope to approach them with grace and dignity. But with unnatural death, with sudden death, with suicide, there is no time to prepare for this loss. We are caught cold. And we are left with questions, questions no one can answer for us.

After the fact, we wonder and we wonder and we wonder. "What if?" we ask. "If only?" we ponder. "Couldn't we have had just one more hour or one more day to talk you out of it?" "Isn't there something that could have been said or done that would have made all this pain and agony unnecessary?" We wonder. We wonder. . . .

In a word, none of us is prepared for sudden and unnatural death. Accidents that kill people are tragedies. Suicides, by comparison, are double tragedies—because, of all sudden deaths, they could have been prevented.

Even though you may, at some level, understand what I have written here there is, in my opinion, no way that you can ever completely prepare those who love you for your suicide. You may try, but you will fail. The most-elaborate notes or explanations or warnings can never comfort the pain those you leave behind will endure. You will be fooling yourself if you think otherwise.

Helen's Story

One mother I worked with had decided to kill herself on Christmas Eve. She had been frustrated and angry with her husband and family and, even on the best of days, her life was just barely tolerable. She was depressed and lonely and felt no one would, or could, listen. Hopeless of ever being understood, her plan was to wait until everyone had gone to bed, take an overdose, and lie down near the presents under the Christmas tree where, she imagined, her family would find her in the morning.

I have heard many suicidal plans but this one, frankly, made me angry and I told Helen so.

"Why are you upset?" she said. "I'm the one who is going to die."

"What are you saying to your family?" I asked.

"That I love them," she said.

"Love them?"

"Well, when I am gone and out of the way, they'll be able to get along much better. They won't have me nagging at them anymore. Don't worry," said Helen, "they'll get over it."

"I hardly think so," I said. "It seems to me you are saying, 'Look what you've done to me! I've killed myself!' And you are saying so in a way they will never forget."

"How?" asked Helen.

"Because they will never have another Christmas that won't be spoiled by your suicide. There will be no cheer in the holiday season or, if there is, it will be a long time coming. Maybe a couple of generations from now they will forget how you died."

Because of her anger, Helen had picked what was traditionally the happiest day of the year for her family on which to kill herself. And only after we talked long and honestly about what this would mean to her husband and children did she come to see and accept that her anger toward them and herself was real and powerful and destructive. I told her that by setting such an example, she was putting a loaded gun into the hands of her children, a gun they might one day point at themselves.

This frightened Helen. "I didn't think . . . ," she said. "I didn't think of it that way."

But as Helen came to understand, in full, what the consequences of her suicide could be to those she said she loved and how her victims would suffer, and how long they would suffer, she began to understand the depth of her anger. Then, with help, she began to do something positive about it. And as she saw things start to change, Helen quit her suicidal plan. With time, her life began to turn around.

Helen, like so many others, was at heart a decent and loving person. But like many others who get caught up in the logic of suicide, she had missed seeing all the parts, all the possible endings, all the consequences. Blinded by her anger and pain, she could not foresee all that would come to pass if she carried through her plan. And when she did begin to see the true damage she could do, she came to realize that she was not just killing herself, but killing the ones she loved as well.

If, by chance, you are thinking as Helen thought and that, for your own reasons, you will kill yourself to get even with someone or to show them that they failed you in some way, then consider what Helen said to me.

"I guess I wanted to hurt them. I wanted them to know how much they were hurting me. I guess I thought that if I left them I could show them how I could hurt them more than they could hurt me. I never thought of killing myself as selfish. Now I know it is."

I can't know your reasons for thinking about suicide. They may make sense to you just now. They might even make sense to me if you could tell them to me. But no matter how good or plausible or reasonable your reasons may be, I hope you will understand that suicide is not a single, quiet thing you do only to yourself. Rather, it is like pulling the pin on a hand grenade while you are surrounded by everyone who knows you.

Yes, some of those people may not like you, some may even hate you; but some of them do care about you and some of them love you. True, you may succeed in killing yourself when you pull the pin, but as surely as the hand grenade explodes, it will send fragments into *all those* around you and they will be victims, too. Innocent ones. For your sake, and theirs, I thought you ought to know.

17 _____ · · ·

Time Heals

If you have read all or most of this book by now, you will have no doubt detected that much of my purpose in writing this book is toward one very simple end — to cause you to stop, to think things through, and to give yourself some time to reconsider the suicide decision. Given the limits of our relationship, I hope I have done that much.

Because, if I have, then I know that there is at least some chance that in the time that has passed since you first picked up this book, your situation may have begun to change. I hope for the better. In the next chapter I will talk to you about how and where you might want to go for professional help if your problems persist, but for the moment, I want to talk to you about time.

I titled this chapter "Time Heals" because time *does* heal. Research conducted on people waiting for counseling or mental health services has demonstrated again and again that, as near as we can tell, the mere passage of time leads to an improvement in their symptoms. Oftentimes, if the person has waited only a week to a few weeks to see a counselor, the reasons he or she was so distressed and requested the appointment will have disappeared and the person no longer wishes to pursue professional help. We call this phenomenon spontaneous recovery.

Spontaneous recovery does not help us explain what happened

to the troubled person and why he is feeling better. He may have shared his problems with a friend, he may have found a job, he may have found someone new to love, he may have quit using drugs on his own, or he may have spoken to his priest or minister and found relief. Frankly, we don't really know why people get better without the professional help they sought. But thank goodness they do.

What we do know is that, as time passes, many troubled people begin to feel better and whatever symptoms they had begin to fade. It may be something the person does for himself or it may be that his circumstances change for the better and those circumstances, in and of themselves, put an end to the crisis.

Maybe it is worthwhile to keep two things in mind. Crises, including suicidal ones, are time-limited. By its very nature, a crisis cannot go on and on and on. Something must give. And, provided you don't kill yourself, something eventually will give. With the simple passage of time things may get worse, but with the same passage of time things may get better. Unless you can know your future perfectly, it seems to me you cannot know with any certainty that, in fact, things will get worse. You may *believe* things will *always* get worse, but that is only a belief, and maybe one of those not-so-rational ones that go with the logic of suicidal thinking.

Ordinary People, Ordinary Problems

The second thing you might want to think about is that the reasons most people give for wanting to kill themselves are not catastrophic. Quite the contrary. For whatever reasons you have been thinking about suicide, and no matter how staggering and unbearable your problems may seem just now, I know that if you could see these same reasons from some point in your own future (from a few weeks to a few months) you would — and I hope will — find them insufficient, maybe even laughable. Many clients have told me after their suicidal crisis passed, "To think—I almost killed myself over that."

The point I want to make is that the reasons most people kill themselves are within the range of ordinary human experience—depression, financial setback, humiliation, unrequited love, the collapse of a marriage, unreasonable pressures at school or work, and all sorts of other hurts and injuries to our self-esteem. But these stresses and losses and experiences of loneliness and depressions and anger have, at bottom, a familiar ring to them—they are all within in the realm of common human experience. You, like me, are not that different from the people I have written about in this book. We all live next door to each other.

So, you might ask, how do we get through these times of crisis in our lives? For whatever comfort you may find in some statistics, it might help to know that studies have shown that as many as fifty percent of the general public (and that's all of us) have *seriously* considered the suicide decision as a solution to a life problem. Other studies have shown that as many as sixty to eighty percent of the entire population have given thought to solving a problem by suicide.

What does this tell us? First, I think these numbers tell us that thinking about suicide is more normal than abnormal. If more than half of the people you pass on the street have at least considered what you are considering, then how different can you be from the rest of us?

But there is something more in these numbers. Question: Why haven't all these people killed themselves?

The answer, I think, lies in the balm of time. The reason most people who think about suicide don't kill themselves is that, even without professional help, they experience some kind of spontaneous recovery. Things change. Their situation changes. The pain they are experiencing diminishes. The hurt and anger ebb away. They get a little help from their friends. They find themselves closer to their God. Someone finally listens to them. They begin to feel a sense of control and mastery return. Something goes right for a change. Any one of a thousand shifts takes place in the currents of their lives. But somehow, sooner or later, the crisis passes, the suicidal thoughts fade and, like a sudden squall on the surface of a lake, the winds stop, the waves quiet down, and a passage opens up where none existed only moments before.

I firmly believe that if you will but put the decision to end your life off, you will, in the days and weeks ahead, find fewer and fewer reasons to choose suicide. What seems so impossible and unbearable today will, in some future place and time, seem only a bad memory. How else, I ask you, can all the millions of people who have given the suicide decision some consideration still be alive?

18   ...

Getting Help

The other day I heard a familiar story. John, a psychologist friend of mine, consults at a university hospital. He described how a young coed had superficially slashed her wrists and then walked across the campus to the emergency room. With blood streaming down both wrists, she said to the nurse on duty, "I think I need help."

She did and she got it. But, John and I wondered, why did she have to slash her wrists first?

I don't know if reading a book like this is going to be helpful to you in the long run, but I hope that what I have to say in this chapter will encourage you to seek help *before* you take some kind of life-threatening action. As a director in a community-based mental-health center, I can assure you that despite how long a waiting list we may have, all those who call us and say they have been thinking about suicide get seen that day or, at worst, the next morning. And, in your own community, this should be true of your crisis clinic, mental-health center or other agency in the business of providing emergency mental-health help. Suicide prevention is one of the primary reasons for our existence.

Your Reluctance

Maybe more than you realize, those of us in the counseling field are aware of how tough it is for any of us to reach out and ask for help. To do so means we have to admit to something that is almost un-American; namely, that we have failed to solve some problem or other on our own. Because of the way we are raised and the way we are taught to be independent and self-healing, asking for help with a crisis in our lives can be a very difficult thing to do. If it is tough for women to ask for help, it is sometimes impossible for men.

Recently I was talking to a young man who had been admitted to a hospital for treatment of his alcoholism. I was asked to see him because he had been thinking about suicide. Sam, a logger by profession, is a good example of how some men feel about getting help.

"Have you ever tried to kill yourself?" I asked.

"Not really," said Sam.

"Not really?"

"Well, I drove my truck off a cliff once." Then he laughed one of those nervous little laughs. "It wasn't a very high cliff."

"Any other attempts?"

"I swam way out in a river once. Dead drunk. But I didn't drown."

"Have you ever asked for help before?" I asked.

"Me? Hell, no! I don't need any help."

And here Sam was, sitting in a hospital, addicted to alcohol, his life in shambles. Sam's life had been running steeply downhill for almost ten years. While intoxicated, he had thought about suicide several times and had gambled with his life more than once. But it never occurred to him to seek help. Or, if he ever did think he might need some help, he sure wasn't going to ask anyone for it—it wouldn't be "manly."

You might think Sam's case is the exception. I don't. I think it's the rule—especially for men. Women, when it comes to asking for help, are far smarter than men.

The point of Sam's story is that he, maybe like you, could not bring himself to pick up the phone and talk to someone about what he was thinking, how he was feeling, and the mess his life had become. Or maybe he thought his problems weren't serious enough. I don't know. But what I do know is that just thinking about suicide is, in my opinion, sufficient reason to ask for help. What other excuse does a person need?

Reaching Out

Almost any community of any size will have something called a help line or hot line or emergency call line or suicide prevention center or mental health center and, usually, their numbers are published on the first page of your local telephone directory. Most smaller communities will list the numbers of crisis lines in neighboring cities. Those numbers are there for a reason. They're there for *you*.

Waiting by those phones twenty-four-hours-a-day are some of America's finest people. Usually trained volunteers working under professional supervision, these good citizens have stepped forward to be available to people just like you: people in crisis, people with problems, people thinking about suicide. I know these volunteers and I know them well. Believe me, they want you to call. It is their whole purpose in giving freely of their time to their community and to you.

In case you may not know it, all calls to such help or crisis lines are completely confidential. You do not even have to give your name. You can, for a quarter, literally call one of these lines and share what has been bothering you with someone who has been trained to listen and to help you sort out the size and shape of your problems and who can, if you need it, refer you to someone or some group that may be just the thing you most need.

This is not to say that once in a while you won't get hold of someone who doesn't seem to be all that helpful. But, if this happens, you can always call back at another time. The point is, don't make a final evaluation of crisis lines because of one poor response on the part of one volunteer. In a word, keep trying.

Professional Help

In case you would like more information about what professional mental-health help is like, what therapy is all about, and would like some guidance about how to find your way to the kind of help that might be best for you, I have written another book on this topic. Titled *The Troubled People Book: A Consumer's Guide to the World of Psychotherapy and Psychotherapists, Continuum, New York, N.Y. 1985*, it is now available in paperback. But here, and so that you'll have at least a little information right now, I will quickly cover the basics and highlight a concern or two I have.

FAMILY PHYSICIANS

Over and over again, we are reminded to see our "family doctor" if we are having problems, including emotional ones. I, personally, consider this generally poor advice for people in an emotional crisis. With some notable exceptions and excluding psychiatrists, most physicians have not had the appropriate training or experience to be of much help to emotionally upset people. Busy professionals, many frequently do not have the time to listen to someone whose life's problems are great and who may be thinking of suicide. Many of them work on a fifteen-minute schedule (that's fifteen minutes per patient) and, as a result, most simply do not have an hour to sit down and listen to someone in trouble.

As a result, and as tragic as it is, many people who commit suicide have recently been treated by their family doctors, sometimes on the same day they take their lives. More to the point, many people who attempt suicide use the very medications supplied to them by their physicians. No doctor I know would willingly supply a lethal dose of medication to a suicidal person.

So, if you go to your family doctor to discuss your problems, you'd better make darn sure you tell him or her that you are having suicidal thoughts and feelings. If he doesn't want to discuss these with you, or gives you the impression he's too busy to listen, or fails to refer you to someone who has the time to listen, then for Pete's sake, get yourself to someone who is trained, has the time, and understands what an emotional and suicidal crisis is.

I know many family physicians. Most of them know exactly what to do if you tell them you're feeling suicidal. Most generally will refer you to a psychiatrist or psychologist they know and respect and, as is their obligation, they will follow up with the doctor they referred you to and see to it that you get the help you need.

So please remember, no physician is a mind reader and, despite how depressed or hopeless you may be feeling, you can't count on your doctor to guess what's going on inside you. Most likely he won't routinely ask you if you are thinking about suicide. So, as tough as it may be, you simply *have* to tell him how you are feeling.

PSYCHIATRISTS

Within the medical profession, psychiatrists are the ones best trained to help you with whatever problems you may be faced with, especially problems that have caused you to begin to think about the suicide decision. Medical doctors first, psychiatrists have completed several years of specialized training in the areas of human behavior. They know all about suicidal thinking and spend most of their professional lives helping people with depression and anger and loneliness and all the other things that make us miserable and unhappy.

Since psychiatrists are the only mental-health professionals with the credentials to prescribe medications and if, for example, you think you may need a medication to counteract a serious depression, then by all means make that first appointment with a psychiatrist or a clinic or community mental-health center where psychiatrists are employed. There is no point in wasting time and money on other kinds of professionals, including other kinds of physicians, if they cannot properly diagnose and treat what is ailing you.

PSYCHOLOGISTS

A psychologist is someone who holds a doctorate in psychology and who, if he or she is offering services to the public, should be licensed by the state. They may be a PhD or an EdD, but in any case they will have specialized in counseling or clinical areas and will have had extensive training and experience in human behavior and the problems associated with living, including suicidal thinking and feelings. Psychologists work in all sorts of settings — hospitals, clinics, private practice — and all of them should have a good working relationship with a psychiatrist or other physician to whom they can refer you for medical evaluation and, if needed, proper medications to help you combat an emotional problem.

SOCIAL WORKERS

Like the other professions I am including here, social workers are a heterogenous group of professional helpers and many or most of them are trained in clinical work. While all social workers are not trained psychotherapists, many of them have specialized in this area and are as competent as any of the other mental-health professionals to help you with your problems. According to their own standards for professional practice, social workers should have a master's degree in social work, state certification (if available in their state), and, ideally, hold membership in the National Academy of Certified Social Workers. This ACSW (Academy of Certified Social Workers) is your best guide to finding a social worker in your community who has all the proper skills and credentials.

PSYCHIATRIC NURSES

Nurses, since the profession began, have been an integral part of the mental health team. More recently, a specialty in psychiatric nursing has developed and more and more nurses with this training are available to help people with problems. A number of nursing schools now offer a master's degree (some even offer a PhD) in psychiatric nursing and, should people like this be available in your community, you can safely bet they will have all the proper training and experience to understand and help you with your crisis.

MASTER'S LEVEL CLINICIANS

There are a large number of schools offering what are called "terminal master's degrees" in the helping professions. These go by many names, but the bottom line is that some of the programs are good and some are not so good. Some states require master's-level therapists to be licensed or certified, others do not. Some of these practitioners may work in clinics or mental-health centers, some may be in private practice. Some may be supervised by PhDs or MDs, others may not. And, while some of these people are excellent therapists, I know of no simple way to guide you to someone who will do a good job for you. (I will suggest how to "triangulate" a good therapist a bit later.)

THE CLERGY

Since many people turn to their priest or minister or clergyman for help, it is important for you to understand that while all clergymen and women know and understand human problems, not all of them will have had special training in counseling. However, more and more clergymen are receiving training and supervision in what is called Clinical Pastoral Counseling and, if you can find someone with this background available in your church or community, then you can be sure you will have found someone able and experienced in helping you with your problems.

This is not to say that if your minister or priest has not had this specialty training, he is inadequate to be of assistance; rather, it just means he has not taken the courses and met the requirements for this certification. Most clergymen I know do a ton of counseling and, when they feel they can't adequately help you with what is bothering you, they will refer you to someone they know who can.

DRUG AND ALCOHOL SPECIALISTS
Most drug and alcohol specialists are broadly trained in human behavior, including what to do to help someone in a suicidal crisis. However, as with any relatively new professional specialty, the training and experience of these counselors is uneven and, therefore, I cannot say that every one of them will be competent to help you with a suicidal crisis. However, if your suicidal thinking and feelings emerge while drinking or drugging or after coming down from a high and you have reason to believe your problems very likely stem from the use or abuse of chemicals, then you will be way ahead by starting out with a drug or alcohol specialist. Also, some psychologists, psychiatrists, social workers, and masters-level therapists will have specialized in chemical dependency and this, if you are having problems with drugs or alcohol, is often the best kind of professional to consult.

Five Steps to Finding a Good Therapist

(1) ASK FOR A REFERRAL
Once you've decided to seek professional help, you'll need the name of someone to contact. A referral is like a recommendation

and the quickest way to get a referral is from someone you know. Ask a friend, call your doctor, talk to someone at a mental health center, or call your crisis line. Many community agencies offer free information and referral services.

I suggest you talk to several people and get a list of names. Most people will give you three names of people they know and respect. You will find, most likely, the same names showing up again and again. These are the people to call—they have the best reputations.

(2) CHECK CREDENTIALS

If you're nervous about accepting a referral and going to see someone, here are a couple of things you can do. One, you can call the professional organization to which they belong (County Medical Society, State Psychological Association, National Association of Social Workers, etc.) to see if the person you are considering is a member in good standing. Secondly, you can call the professional and interview him or her on the phone. This may feel a bit awkward, but if you have questions about his or her affiliations, credentials, training and such, then by all means ask those questions. Most therapists are happy to answer such inquiries. If they are not, keep looking.

(3) ASK ABOUT THE THERAPIST'S APPROACH OR STYLE

If, like most people, you are unsure about what you are getting into by seeing a therapist, feel free to ask all the questions you have while you have them on the phone. It may help to jot your questions down before making the call. Will you be seen alone or with your spouse or family? What kind of therapy does the therapist practice? How much does it cost? I'm not suggesting you keep him or her on the phone for thirty minutes, but I am suggesting you get all the answers you need to feel comfortable about going for that first appointment.

(4) ASK THAT THE FIRST VISIT BE A CONSULTATION

Rather than make a commitment to ongoing therapy, it is sometimes wise to ask for the first appointment to be a consultation. Some therapists do not charge for this first visit. A consultation is different from therapy in that neither you nor the therapist is making a commitment to a series of therapy sessions. Rather, it is an hour during which each of you can decide if the other is someone you can work with. It is a step I strongly recommend. Not everyone likes everyone on a first meeting and a poor connection for therapy can be worse than no therapy at all.

(5) IF IN DOUBT, GET A SECOND OPINION

Having secured a list of therapists and having interviewed and been interviewed by one, you may feel the two of you did not have a good take. If this happens, then by all means seek a second opinion. If you left that first appointment feeling uncertain that the therapist could help you (or that he or she was cold or indifferent or too peculiar or too anything), then call the next person on your list. Your life is just too important not to be cautious in this phase of getting the help you need.

What Kind of Professional?

Almost everyone not familiar with the broad spectrum of mental health professionals will, once they decide to seek help, ask the question: "Who should I see?" I wish I had an easy answer but, frankly, the world of therapists is a confusing one.

However, a general rule of thumb is that the more serious your problems, the more training your therapist should have. If you are suffering from a serious depression, unstable mood swings, or emotional problems that are preventing you from working or going to school (and especially if some kind of medication is indicated), then you should start with a psychiatrist. If seeing a psychiatrist privately is too expensive, then contact a mental-health center or an outpatient clinic where psychiatrists work.

In my experience, however, most qualified therapists know when you need the attention of a psychiatrist and, even if you begin with someone who is not a psychiatrist, they will refer you on for an evaluation and possible medications.

Unfortunately for the consumer, much of the conflict and confusion in the mental-health field stems from quarrels among us professionals as to who is qualified to do what with whom and for how long and for how much. Maybe it helps to keep in mind that these are relatively new professions and that, as yet, we haven't sorted everything out. But the point I most want you to remember is that, despite our differences, all of us who have been in this field any length of time are familiar with suicidal thoughts and feelings and know what to do to help you through whatever crisis you may be in.

Finally, I do not believe that everyone who goes through a suicidal crisis needs professional help. There are dozens of things you can do for yourself without professional guidance. You can exercise, take better care of yourself through diet and nutrition, seek spiritual answers from your church, your God, or through meditation. You can join self-help groups that are working on problems just like yours. You can read self-help books and undertake a host of self-improvement projects that may change both the direction and quality of your life. You can change damaging relationships, quit booze or drugs, and otherwise begin to take better care of yourself.

But if these things fail, then please remember we volunteers and professionals are there in the wings—waiting for your call. And I mean, literally, day or night.

19   ...

A Philosophy of Life

I can't know whether or not you have a philosophy of life. But maybe, if you've been thinking about the suicide decision, you don't. Maybe, because life has seemed so unbearable lately, your beliefs in what is positive and valuable and worthwhile about life have been shattered. Maybe, in this dark hour, you are having trouble finding a purpose, a meaning, a reason to go on living. I don't know how it is with you and, unless we meet somewhere sometime, there is no way I can.

But having worked with many people like yourself, I know for certain that one of the things we most need to see us through the tough times is a belief that life, despite its pain and disappointments is, in the final analysis, better than whatever death holds for us. And this belief, however we put words or actions to it, is our philosophy of life.

I don't know when or how one develops a philosophy of life. I am not sure how one comes to own a particular set of values or ideas or convictions or principles or whatever you choose to call those beliefs around which our lives turn more or less smoothly, but somehow, as we add one year upon another, I believe all of us come to some reckoning of our unique place in humanity, in the world, and in the cosmos. And, at least from my point of view, without knowing this place, we are never quite complete, can never be quite content, and can never feel entirely at peace in this sometimes crazy and painful world.

More importantly, without knowing in what we truly believe, we are like blades of grass—easily blown one way or another in the winds of a crisis. Without a central core of firm beliefs or faith in ourselves or in our God, we can become the victims of our own self-doubt, the victims of our own emotions and, yes, the victims of our own hostility or hopelessness.

I have often thought that much of what a client derives from seeing a therapist has less to do with what the therapist does, than with what he or she believes—which is why I have encouraged young therapists to be positive about life, about the human spirit, and about man's ability to rise above his circumstances and to change his life for the better. If a therapist is not hopeful, how can a client be? If a therapist does not affirm the value of life and make strong arguments against death and suicide, how can the sufferer?

When I began writing this book, I read all I could about the ethics of suicide—the case for rational suicide, the case for letting people kill themselves if they so wished, the case that therapists have or do not have the right to impose their beliefs on others or to intervene or not intervene with the force of law to prevent someone from killing himself. And as I read this material, I was struck that much of what the experts have to say on this subject is no more or less than the expression of their personal philosophies of life—its value, its sanctity, its purpose, its utility to others or to the future of mankind.

This, I suppose, is how it should be in the world of ethics and philosophy. As I'm not an expert, I don't know. But my reading did make one thing clear: In my work with suicidal people I have decided that once someone has come into my office and entered my frame of reference, they have entered my value system, my personal and, yes, philosophical world. And therefore, as a counselor and healer, my decision will always be to do all I can to prevent what I consider to be an unnecessary act of suicide.

Since you have read most of this book, I suppose in a way I have tricked you. Maybe, before you began to read what I have written, you were hoping to find some justification from me that your life was, truly, not worth living. And now you find, in the last chapter, that I offered no such justifications and that I am an enemy of the suicide decision in almost every single circumstance. I hope you do not feel tricked, but if you do, I hope you will see my purpose as I intended it—and that purpose is in keeping with what I believe: To keep you alive until you find your own reasons to live.

So, at the close of this book, I am going to ask you to think about your philosophy of life or, if you feel you do not have one, to consider that you might need one now—that you need to find some new reasons to live. For I am convinced that if you will but take the time to examine your life, your goals, your good traits and your bad, your accomplishments and your failures, that you will be the stronger for the effort and that that strength, that self-knowledge, once you have gained it, is the best defense against ending your life by suicide.

I do not think it is possible to live many more than a dozen years and not develop some beliefs about what life is all about and what it means to be a human being. And so, no matter what your age may be now, I believe you have and hold some things to be true and that, though you may not think so, you do have something of a philosophy of life already. These may be religious beliefs, spiritual beliefs, beliefs about how people are, how they act, and how they "should" treat one another. And I believe you already know a great deal about yourself.

The question, then, is not whether you have a philosophy of life, but rather that you may need to expand upon the one you have; enrich it, nurture it some way so that your philosophy of life becomes a great flywheel that spins and spins and spins and carries you through the bad times. Not to come to know what you believe in and, thereby, what your life means is, maybe, to start to dwell upon your own death and how to achieve it. The idea of our own death by suicide may get us around and through the long and lonely nights, but it is our dreams of what tomorrow can be that make the days endurable and worthwhile. As someone once said: Without our dreams, we die.

My own philosophy of life is not important. And though I have thought long and hard about what I believe, I would not ask that anyone see things the way I do, or feel things the way I feel them, or come to the same conclusions I have come to about the human condition and what it means to be a member of the species. My philosophy is mine and while it may be shared by some, it is not shared by all. Nor would I expect it to be. What is important for me is that I have a personal philosophy and that, when the hard decisions have to be made, I can make them with some sense of internal consistency, with a feeling that I am acting on principles that I have come to call my own. They may be right or they may be wrong, but I am willing to own them and say of them that they are what make me who, not what, I am.

Give Yourself a Gift

What I would ask of you now is that you give yourself a very precious gift. And that gift is this: The time, the space, and the solitude to begin to sort out what it means to you to be a human being and to have a life to live. Admittedly, this is a spiritual quest, even an existential one. And, some might argue, a psychologist hasn't much business mucking around with things philosophical or religious or spiritual.

But what others think about me at this moment doesn't really matter. What matters is that I hold true to what I believe, and one of those beliefs is that I feel strongly that if you will begin to look inward and begin that difficult search for who you are, you will be the stronger for it.

At this, maybe the most troubled time in your life, I realize that such a search is going to be difficult. But it is too easy, I think, for all of us to simply accept the beliefs of others as our own. We live in a time of fast foods and convenience stores and cute quips that pass for wisdom and, I have sometimes wondered, if we are not all the victims of a fast-lane mentality that makes simple solutions like suicide easier than struggling with our own thoughts and fears and doubts and learning to sacrifice for love rather than to expect it to be given us with a money back guarantee.

You have no doubt heard the now-popular saying, "Life is a bitch, and then you die." It is a clever one-liner and making the rounds just now. But is it true? Is it true for you? When things have not been going right in my world, I have repeated this little phrase myself. But these eight words are a powerful and negative statement about life and while I may make a joke with them from time to time, I do not really believe them to be true for me at all times and under all circumstances. Quite the opposite. I could just as well say, "Life is a picnic, but sometimes you get ants."

The first one-liner justifies my occasional pessimism, the second challenges me to see a bigger picture. It is up to me to choose between them. I make that choice—consciously, daily. I would ask that you do the same for yourself.

My point here is that however we come to believe something, it is important that we stop, think, and decide whether we truly believe what we are saying. Because when the suicide decision starts running around in our heads, is it not too easy to avoid the hard questions and opt out of the only life we have? Is it not too easy to say to ourselves that, if "Life is a bitch, and then you die . . . then why not die now and get it over with?" Because if it is, it is too simple. Too slick. Too pat. It is a dime's worth of philosophy in a million-dollar world.

So, I would ask you, is it not time to do some of the hard things for yourself, to begin to ask some of the difficult questions of yourself? Is it not time to learn who you are and to come to know what you believe in? If you are like the rest of us, you won't like some of what you see in the mirror. But, so what—they're saving perfection for us in the next life.

Right now we've got to get along with the bumps and pimples, the bad habits, the weaknesses, the failings, the ugly little aspects of our character that we'd rather be without but that seem to stick to us like tar. Right now we, all of us, need to get on better terms with ourselves so that, despite our imperfections, we can get going with what is good and valuable and worthwhile and learn to stop hurting ourselves and those we love.

It will not come as chilling news to you that no one gets out of this life alive and that, while we are here, we need something to believe in to keep us going. I don't know what this needs to be for you or where you will find it, but I know that if you will but look you will find something, something worth living for, some reason to put one foot in front of the other until a better day arrives.

I will confess and share with you that some of the longest therapy hours I have spent have been with suicidal people who were utterly convinced that their lives were essentially finished and the only thing left that needed doing was to get the dying over with. They could not, despite all their efforts and mine, find a way in which to feel good about staying alive. But, because they didn't quit and I didn't quit, we made it through. And, in time, things got sorted out and we (and I mean *we*) survived.

I will tell you what I have often told others who were in the midst of a suicidal crisis and who were searching for some reason to go on. They, maybe like you, felt lost and hopeless and as if nothing held any promise for them. They did not have a faith in some higher power to sustain them. And, despite how much I would like to have infected them with my zest for living and my philosophy of life, this is not an easy thing to do. Because, for all the reasons a person enters a suicidal crisis, it is not a state of mind easily switched around by another's optimism. And so, as a way to find a common ground to bide the time, I have told this story.

I have told them that we are as two people on a ship that is lost at sea and, so far as we can know, the captain has fallen overboard and no one is at the helm. The radio is out. There is a heavy fog all around us and no one can see where we are bound. We can see no beacon of light from a friendly shore. We can hear no sound of a rescue ship. One of us is terribly frightened. The other of us (me), is also frightened—but a bit less so. I am a little less frightened because I have something to do to keep me busy. I have a job to do.

My job is to give comfort until we are found or until the fog clears away and we can both see clearly again. But this is a two-way relationship. For me to feel good about giving support and comfort and encouragement, I need you to be willing to hang on—not to jump overboard because your fear of the unknown is greater than your fear of the here and now.

And so, together, we will share our fear. And in this sharing we will come to know each other. We will talk and joke and tell stories and be kind to each other. We may not soon be rescued and may never be, but while we are lost, we will be together and, together, our fears will subside and we will have a purpose in our being.

I hope, now that you have read this book, that you will do for yourself what you must do to keep going—to reach out, to make that telephone call, to talk to someone you know and respect, to seek out a therapist, to find your way back to God, or whatever it is that you need to do to end your isolation and suffering. If you will do this, now, today, and give yourself the time it takes for the fog to lift and the crisis to pass, then I know you will make it and I will feel nothing short of wonderful for having shared this time with you.

I wish to leave you with one thought. It is from the Talmud.

"Whoever preserves one life, it is as if he preserved an entire world."

By choosing to live, you can be that person.

Epilogue

Since *Suicide: The Forever Decision* was first published many things have happened. The world itself has changed. The Berlin Wall has fallen. A war has come and gone. The autoimmune-deficiency virus known as AIDS has struck a new kind of terror into the hearts of people everywhere and, suddenly, our beliefs about the sanctity of life have been thrown under the bright light of reexamination. Recent advances in modern medicine are nothing short of miraculous and, while people still die naturally, the possibilities for extending the days, months, and years available to us are staggering.

But, many now ask, at what price? And with what quality of life?

As free choice is the very definition of liberty, there are those here in America and elsewhere who now wish to extend the definition of freedom to the taking of one's own life—with or without the legal assistance of a physician. The success of the recent book *Final Exit* by Derek Humphry of the Hemlock Society (a how-to book on suicide) suggests that there are many thousands of people who feel a need for this information.

As I cannot know the minds of the people who are buying Mr. Humphry's book, it is my guess that the great majority of them are intelligent people who, knowing that there may come a time in their own lives when, faced with the certain reality of a slow, painful, expensive, and undignified death, they may choose to make the forever decision. For the truly dying, and because this is such a deeply personal matter, I do not feel it is my place, personally or professionally, to proffer logical, clinical, or even moral arguments against such carefully considered action.

But as a psychologist who has worked with hundreds of suicidal people, I am also painfully aware that depression is the common cold of our society, that even untreated depressions lift, that therapy works, that our society's insidious ageism (believed so by the elderly as well as the young) inspires self-destruction, and that the great majority of the problems over which people end their lives are not the extraordinary ones of facing a certain and painful death, but the ordinary ones of broken hearts and shattered dreams. Even the most savage hopelessness passes, sometimes with no more than the balm of time.

Since the publication of this book, I have received many letters from readers who, while their excerpted thoughts must remain anonymous here, may help you understand how important it is to give yourself some time—time to understand, to rest, to learn, to reconsider, to heal and to carry on until another tomorrow.

—I've been thinking about suicide for some time now and the one thing holding me back is the thought of perhaps failing at the attempt. Are there really more failed attempts than complete suicides? I must be mighty stupid in not having the confidence in myself concerning taking my life. So many people indeed succeed. If I knew that I'd be successful in taking my life, I surely wouldn't be writing now, nor would I have read your book.

—June 15 of this year I was calmly working out the details of my suicide when I remembered your book, which I had not read. So I read it . . . all night. I am writing to tell you that you may have saved my life. As promised in your book, the very next day a friend called from Arizona to tell me he was coming for a visit. I'm going to get some help now. Thank you for the hope and courage to keep going.

—I feel I know you. I went to the library today looking for books about near-death experiences to support my feelings about ending my life. None of those books was available, but to make a long story short, I spent the afternoon reading your book *Suicide: The Forever Decision.* I felt compelled to read the whole book. I guess you accomplished your goal in that I postponed my suicide another day or so. So far as ending my misery, I guess I'm not quite there yet.

—I purchased your book *Suicide* in January 1988. At that time it did prevent me from taking my life. Two months later I didn't think to look at it before overdosing. Twice more in '88 I again ignored your wise counsel and spent time in a critical-care unit. In spite of my past and possible future attempts at self-harm, I believe your book is the best-written on the subject. . . . Thanks for sharing a part of yourself with others. I appreciate it.

—I was afraid if I kept reading I would get the urge to go ahead and take my life. But after reading the whole book I won't say I'm cured, but I feel much better. I'm going to give it to my counselor to read.

—I just thought I would write you a letter telling you that I appreciate the honesty in your book. I attempted suicide in June and told myself that in January I would kill myself and make sure I did it right this time. But I made the decision to live yesterday. I will turn the gun (my father's .22) over to my psychiatrist on October 6. Your book pointed a lot out to me. I believe there is something better for me and I'm gonna fight like hell to get it.

—I won't tell you my life story, but I will tell you I attempted suicide and that I thought I had the knowledge to overdose (I'm a nurse). The dosage I took should have worked, but I'm still alive. I'm going to read your book over again. As this is Christmas Eve, thank you for the best Christmas present—your insight, your hope, and encouragement.

—I really enjoyed your book. My feelings about suicide frequently go back and forth. I bought your book the same night I bought a bottle of Tylenol. I decided to read your book first. And when I finished it, do you know what I did? I flushed the pills down the toilet. Reading your book first was probably one of the smartest things I've done in a long time. I just wanted to let you know that it helped.

Finally, it is my hope that after reading this book and these letters you, too, can find a way to give yourself the gift of life.